# Small Urban Manufacturers

Artisans of our times that
Chun Soon-ok has ever met

# 소공인

# Small Urban Manufacturers

Artisans of our times that
Chun Soon-ok has ever met

Chun Soon-ok · Kwon Eun-jeong
translated by Chun Soon-ok

뿌리와
이파리
**PURIWA IPARI**

# Finding fresh hope in small urban manufacturers

This book is a sequel to *They Are Not Machines* (Ashgate, 2003), which focuses on the lives and struggles of Korean women workers who worked in manufacturing in the 1960s and the 1970s. Impoverished by Japanese occupation (1910-1945) and the Korean War (1950-1953), Korea had turned into one of the poorest countries in the world, with the gross national income per capita amounting to a meager USD 67 by 1953. However, the compressed and astonishing industrialization of the country in the following two decades kept the national economy growing at almost 10 percent a year. The abrupt expansion of the Korean economy made the country export USD 10 billion worth of goods in cumulative total by 1977, helping it achieve the so-called Miracle of the Han River and setting an example for other developing economies worldwide.

*They Are Not Machines* features the hidden and untold stories of the suffering, alienation and solidarity of women workers in Korea without whom the nation's economic transformation would not have been possible. Born and raised in abject poverty and facing discrimination against women from birth onward, young teenage girls in Korea were forced to work for next-to-nothing pays in countless shops and factories of light manufacturing, producing textiles, apparel, wigs, leather goods and shoes that led Korea's industrialization. These poor girls worked under the low ceilings of barely lit and poorly ventilated sweatshops, and were denied even the chances to make the needed trips to bathrooms. furthermore, they worked tirelessly for 98 hours a week for pays that were far below the national minimum wage level.

I, myself, began working at a sweatshop at the age of 16, and continued to work in the clothes-making and leather goods shops at the Pyeonghwa Market for seven years afterward. I was personally familiar with the miserable working conditions and lives of women my age. Shortly after I became acquainted with labour activism, in November 1970, a tragic event occurred that accelerated the spread of unionism throughout Korea: namely, the self-immolation of Chun Tae-il, my own elder brother and a fellow worker of the Pyeonghwa Market, who poured gasoline over and lit himself, demanding that factory owners abide by the Labour Standards Act and shouting that we were not machines. He lived an all too brief span of 22 years. But his death awakened society from its willful blindness about the dire conditions facing workers and raised the public awareness of workers' rights. His self-immolation also served to unite the workers of the Pyeonghwa Market into forming the Cheonggye Union, which went onto play a pivotal role in labour activism, solidarity and the democratization movement in Korea.

I bore witness to the entire process. Koreans finally achieved the direct presidential election system in June 1987 after years of struggle for democratization. In the following July through September, labour strikes were held nationwide to win the government's authorization on the creation of democratic labour unions, pay raises and working environment improvements. After a brief break, the democratization groups in Korea entered debates of growing intensity over where they should be headed in the future. Having realized the importance of achieving solidarity with the labour unions of other countries around the world, I decided to learn about the wider world. In 1989, I left for the United Kingdom, and studied comparative labour relations of Europe and the sociology of labour. In 2001, I finally published my doctoral dissertation, entitled *They Are Not Machines*, undeniably taken from the words of my dying brother.

In 1998, I returned to Korea briefly to do field work for my dissertation. During those five months, one question gripped me. Korean society has been developing at a rapid pace since 1970, but why do workers still face the same living conditions? Why do these makers of the Miracle of the Han River have nothing in their hands now? Since I returned to my home country for good in 2001, I have spent the last 11 years looking for an answer.

While looking for the answer, I realized that I could help these workers better with practical research and actions than by immersing myself in theoretical concerns. I went to Dongdaemun, the hub of the textile and garment industry in Korea, and launched various activities to support seamstresses there. I set up an after school facility for the children of working mothers and a study centre for female advanced machinist. I also founded Suda Gongbang, a technical training center for women workers, and co-founded a social enterprise with its highly-skilled graduates.

In 2012, I was selected as a proportional representative of the National Assembly. I felt it was my duty on the small urban manufacturers('SUM') who had contributed to the Miracle on the Han River and endured dreadful working conditions in the 1970s and 1980s, when Korea was busy industrializing. Despite their contributions, these small urban manufacturers have been forgotten by society and became invisible to policymakers. I took it as my mission to establish proper laws and institutions for these small urban manufacturers and their employees.

The global financial crisis, which broke out in 2008, has gone through such restructure process in numerous economies worldwide. According to the Statistics Korea, the current unemployment rate among young people in Korea stands at a very worrying 10.7 percent. Most of the incumbent administration's policies directed toward raising the employment rate to 70 percent focus only on service providers and the so-called "future growth-engine industries." However, around the country today, small urban manufacturers such as those producing shoes, bags, eyeglasses, jewelry and accessories, as well as printing and metalworking shops number around 310,000 and employ over 1,500,000 people. Between 2006 and 2012, their numbers have increased. Mostly clustered around city centers, they are high-skilled, labour-intensive manufacturers usually employing not more than ten people. They are effective at creating and retaining jobs.

The problem is that SUMs face practical limitations such as its aging workforce. Because SUMs have been neglected by policy makers for so long, I felt the need to develop across-the-board support measures, rather than short-term peripheral solutions for them. In an effort to explore the rationale for providing them with institutional and political support, I conducted a nationwide survey of SUMs. Based on the survey results, I organized several public forums and meetings, and visited neighborhoods with clusters of SUMs to speak with workers in the field. Then, after brainstorming and sharing ideas with legal and public policy experts, I sponsored a bill that became the "Special Act on Support for Small Urban Manufacturers." I prepared, proposed, and submitted the bill to the plenary session at the National Assembly. The bill became law on May 29, 2015. While preparing the bill, I would dream of turning downtown alleyways into homes for artisans, who would breathe life and vitality into the twisting lanes. I realized that to turn this dream into reality, I needed to explain to many people, especially the youth, just how nice it is to be an artisan. It was in that vein that I interviewed artisans from many SUMs of different trades, and from them I learned the history of their specializations and what it means to live as an artisan in this country.

My previous work, *They Are Not Machines*, was my PhD dissertation at the University of Warwick in 2001 and was made into a book, published in the United Kingdom and the United States, on strong recommendations from my supervisor and labour experts. This was not only because of the importance of the subject matter, but also because of its unique approach to research. Whereas similar research projects focus mainly on statistics and reinterpreting their possible meanings, but my work based on the oral records of interviews with Korean workers. Numerous scholars, Korean and otherwise, have been writing and publishing on the topic of Korea's economic miracle, but few had turned their attention to the role of poorly paid and undereducated Korean workers, treating them as merely secondary to Korea's transformation. I believe, however, that we will never begin to understand what the economic growth has truly meant and entailed in Korea without studying in detail what kind of sacrifices went into making that growth possible and how the fruit of that growth has been shared.

That was why I strove to learn from women workers, who have lived through the tumultuous decade of the 1970s in Korea, about the dual structure of oppression — targeting workers and women — they faced, and how the political, judicial and economic powers of the day legitimized and institutionalized the exploitation and repression of these workers.

This book follows the lives of workers who were in their 10s and 20s in the 1970s and tells the story of how they have lived and worked in the past four decades after having played central role during the heyday of Korea's industrialization. In choosing the interviewees for this project, I applied the following criteria:

1. They are working, at the time of the interview, in the traditional areas of small urban manufacturing, such as dressmaking, shoemaking, bag making and jewelry.

2. They have been working for more than 30 years at the time of the interview and attained to a certain level of mastery over their respective arts.

3. They are imparting, at the time of the interview, their knowledge and skills to successive generations of aspiring artisans in any way possible.

There were dozens of candidates who satisfied these criteria, so I carefully selected ten of them. From October 2013 to August 2015, I visited the chosen interviewees at their respective workplaces and interviewed them about the details of their work and lives.

I myself worked as a seamstress in sweatshops in the 1970s. My experience in labour activism in the 1980s and working with women seamstresses for 11 years since 2001, and my encounters with craftspeople and artisans of diverse trades after becoming a politician in 2012, have given me more than enough chances to discover the real gems of small manufacturing industries.

I have a friend who grew up in urban slums and began working as a seamstress' assistant at the age of 14, and dedicated the prime of her life to labour activism with the Cheonggye Apparel Labour Union, before she finally discovered the delight of wholehearted dressmaking. I also became acquainted with a master bag maker who has learned, through four decades of work, that only truly happy craftspeople can make quality products. I also befriended a master dressmaker who used to be ashamed of her job when she was young, but who now takes pride in her profession as among the most valuable lines of work in the world. I happened to meet a master shoemaker who would not trade five decades of his work for a degree from the most prestigious university in the world.

Each of them has progressed from being a common craftsman to an artisan, relying solely on their manual skills. They are a pillar of the Korean economy, supporting it from the bottom up. That is why it is important to shed light on their lives. It is also necessary to develop the means to ensure that they can pass down their valuable skills and know-how to the next generation, while they are still in the field. They may not have been treated well by society, but they are living proof that, while lifetime employment may not exist, there is such a thing as a lifelong job. I truly hope this book helps them create a sustainable environment where they can pass down their skills and wisdom to the next generation, not to mention an environment in which young people can envision a future working in small urban manufacturing.

If someone were to ask me what my dream is, I would say that I am dreaming of a country where work is not drudgery, which workers do not have to endure in the throes of forced passion; a country where work is a learning, liberating, and life-changing experience; a country where everyone's workplace is fun and exciting; a country where aging is not viewed with anxiety and fear, but as a natural process of moving toward the completion of one's life. It is this desire to achieve that kind of country in Korea that has led me to look for, discover and listen to the stories of master artisans who have borne witnesses to Korea's transformation with their own lives.

It is not that Korea lacks the kind of skilled and proud artisans that have made the reputations of Chanel, Prada and A. Testoni possible. Korea has even better skilled artisans, but they remain hidden from the global spotlight because of the public and policymakers' neglect. Now that Korea is about to join the league of the wealthiest nations with gross national income per capita of over USD 30,000, we have the important task of translating the slogan of the 1970s, "We are not machines," to "We are not mere technicians." That is how we inherit and keep alive the spirit of Chun Tae-il.

Last but not least, I would like to express my gratitude and respect to the interviewees who took time out of their busy day and openly shared many intimate details of their experiences. They are neither celebrities nor people who have achieved legendary success. However, I believe that if you are a perceptive reader, you can read between the lines and hear their unspoken stories from their blunt, stubby hands, calloused from a lifetime of hard labour, and from their creases and furrows that almost resemble tree rings, evidence of the emotional journeys their work has taken them on.

From Yeouido in March 2016
Chun Soon-ok 전순옥

# Table of Contents

## Chapter 2 Can we just get a word?

## Chapter 3 Crafts contained the breath of their makers will be forever

**| Explanatory Notes |**

- Interviews and symposiums in this book were held between October 2013 and August 2015.
- Ten artisans' brief biographies and years of work experiences were dated back from 2015.
- *'Shida'* is a slang word for seamstress's assistant or apprentice. This word, commonly used by the interviewees in the field, were left untranslated throughout the book.

# The solution in the field[*]

I began writing this book in autumn of 2013. In October of that year, when I was about to sponsor a bill before the National Assembly that later became the Special Act on Support for Small Urban Manufacturers (the "Act"), I started to write an interview series for *Pressian*. I called it the "D Project of Chun Soon-ok and Kwon Eun-jeong."

Though the "D" in the name comes from Dongdaemun, the quintessence of Korea's clothes and sewing industry, the project was meant to draw attention to artisans of all kinds of small-scale manufacturers, including shoemakers and bag makers, shining a light on the value and importance of small urban manufacturers ("SUMs").

To promote the value of the D Project and the necessity of the Act, I volunteered to be the first interviewee. From there, we held a series of 12 interviews that continued until March 2014. We met with artisans as well as policy experts who studied the economics of SUMs and explored ways to foster them. After wrapping up the interviews, I continued to track down and interview artisans working in a broader range of manufacturing fields, including accessories, jewelry, and clothes. It was these discoveries that led me to pen this book.

Six seasons came and went by while I was preparing this book. During that time, the Act, co-sponsored by 88 lawmakers from both the ruling and the opposition parties, took effect in December 2013. The Act is an invaluable outcome, a crystallization of my philosophy that "labor is the solution, and the solution is in the field." One term found throughout the book is "small urban manufacturers." I met Kwon Eun-jeong, this book's co-author, again to explain what SUMs are, why they are important, why I scrutinized issues relating to them, and how I developed valuable relationships with the artisans highlighted in this book.

---

\*   This interview was held in October 2013 before 'Special Act on Support for Small Urban Manufacturers' was ratified. This law was passed by the National Assembly and has been implemented since May 2015.

# Who says manufacturing is a sunset industry?

In September 2013, a public hearing on the Act was held in the council chamber of the National Assembly Research Service. The room was crowded with workers from all types of small manufacturing firms whose eyes were filled with hope for the 'card' presented by Ms. Chun. They had always thought the law was just something to be followed, not something that could be shaped by them. However, when a law becomes a matter that affects your own household, it is no longer a cold term that conjures up thoughts of *Crime and Punishment*; it becomes a warm-blooded living thing. The Act felt that way to Ms. Chun, too. To her, it was a creature that needed to be born, a child-like organism that needed to be nurtured and tenderly cared for after its birth.

Says Ms. Chun: "This is the solution I reached after many trips to the field over lengthy period of time. Most of the places I visited were in the basement of some old building or were small factories hidden in the neglected corners of a building. These small manufacturers usually have two or three technicians but no more than ten. A lot of the technicians in such businesses have three or four decades of experience, and are such talented craftsmen that it would be fair to call them artisans or virtuosos. These businesses number over 300,000 around the country, and they employ more than 600,000 people in Korea's seven largest cities alone. That is a huge industry, but the government has never paid much attention to them. Given that so many people have been running these businesses for decades, isn't it obvious that the government should care about them? There should have already been a law in place. This Act is designed to create a sustainable environment for these manufacturers and provide them with comprehensive support."

She cites the reasons that she believes working conditions at SUMs have seen little to no improvement for decades:

"Mass production systems were an important driver behind Korea's rapid industrial growth, and until the 1980s, Korea had many large factories. But beginning around 1987, labor-intensive manufacturers moved to China, Vietnam, and other countries with lower labor costs. Around that time, the growing number of technicians who had lost their jobs set up small factories in the basements of buildings and ran them with their wives. Such factories need to produce goods as soon as orders are placed. That's the nature of the business. So they have to be located in cities. They are small family-run businesses or micro-enterprises with an average of five employees. Because of their small size and scarcity of labor unions, SUMs have been largely neglected by policy makers."

One might say that the starting point of the Act was Dongdaemun. When you think of Dongdaemun, the clothes merchants or "Dongdaemun fashion" come to mind. Indeed, Dongdaemun is a fashion hub, home to 70 percent of Korea's fashion businesses. Over 10,000 sewing factories and 39,000 fashion distributors cling to it, giving jobs to 120,000 people. Dongdaemun is perhaps the only market in the world to offer one-stop service, from taking orders to manufacturing and distribution. To be specific, it is a cluster of some 80,000 fashion businesses, attracting about 600,000 people a day. Its infrastructure is ideally suited for the fast-changing fashion trends currently sweeping the world.

Even if it didn't boast all these assets, Ms. Chun considers Dongdaemun worthy of her life's dedication. Her family history is wrapped up in here, and it would not be an exaggeration to say that her family embodies Korea's modern history. The people of Dongdaemun are like her siblings, and Dongdaemun represents their livelihood as well as their lifeline. She instinctively senses that

"*Developing the industry and ensuring more respect for craftsmen is important. Then, they can evolve into high value-added brand name products.*"

developing the clothing and sewing industry and helping them prosper is her duty. Her mission is to construct a proper work environment so that everyone there can reap and share the fruits of their labor.

However, the fast pace of global fashion trends is triggering rapid changes in Korea's market landscape. Local clothing and sewing businesses are being cornered by global brands and larger clothing companies and distributors whose goal is to "sell it all fast and cheap."

Ms. Chun says her mind is racing:

"Today, hundreds of thousands of factories are vanishing. The manufacturing ecosystem is falling apart. And it's not going to hold up much longer if we don't restructure it soon. I decided to draft the bill because I felt they [factories] could no longer be neglected. I believe that if this Act is enforced, it will usher in a new paradigm for the industry. More importantly, it will give people vision and hope. Because they have been ignored by policy makers for so long, they feel empowered knowing that a new law has been enacted just for them. They are heartened knowing they can further develop their businesses and update their technologies."

This means that people in the trades feel the Act is there to work for them, which is having a positive effect on their sense of worth and hope for the future:

"Developing the industry and ensuring more respect for craftsmen is important. If that happens, the products they create will be compared to those made by artisans as opposed to blue-collar laborers. In other words, they can evolve into high value-added brand name products. Then these craftsmen, beaming with pride, will want to keep honing their skills and making quality goods under their name. This can be a key to revitalizing Korea's small-scale manufacturing sector."

# This is how we change the future for SUMs

—

What types of assistance does the Act provide?

"It makes tax benefits available. It also enables the government to set up training systems designed to provide factories with skilled workers. Moreover, if at least 50 factories producing the same types of goods are located within a certain geographic boundary, that area can be designated a "small urban manufacturers' cluster," and linked to a dedicated assistance center that provides local SUMs with important services. The Act also furnishes financial support for building vital infrastructure and renovating run-down factory facilities. One of the most important support mechanisms is the creation of a joint marketing system. Most SUMs in the sewing business are subcontractors. If they can come together to open a cooperative store to sell their goods, the clothing industry can achieve remarkable growth. As part of this program, I received some funding from the National Assembly's Trade, Industry & Energy Committee ("TIEC") and used it to launch a clothes accessories showroom called "LEDOME." It is designed to showcase and sell clothes, shoes, bags, jewelry and art made by fashion-based SUMs as well as by emerging designers who previously had no place to show off their wonderful ideas and planning abilities. With this channel, they can now receive orders from Korea and abroad, and produce samples and actual goods by collaborating with nearby factories."

Some changes were made as the bill wended its way through the review and approval process. The bill was originally designed to divide SUMs in Korea's seven largest cities — Seoul, Busan, Daegu, Gwangju, Incheon, Daejeon and Ulsan — into regional economic "belts." But during the plenary session on the bill, the areas covered were expanded to include the entire country. In the Act's name, the word "Downtown" was changed to "Urban." And in the process of shaping the bill's final form, the scope of businesses and industries covered by the Act grew. Beginning in early 2013, Ms. Chun conducted a nationwide survey of small manufacturers to collect accurate data that could be used to assess the competitiveness and potential of Korea's small-scale manufacturing sector. In the end, the Act's reach was broadened to embrace all types of businesses clustered in downtowns, from makers of handmade shoes, bags, eyeglasses, jewelry, and fashion accessories to printing and metal-working shops and clothing and sewing businesses.

"It can be honestly said that the Act covers any and all things that can be made by hand. These are conventional industries that rely on both manual skills and machine operation. Under the Act, among the "high-skilled labor-intensive manufacturers that tend to gather in certain areas," those with 10 workers or less are eligible for support. The biggest problem facing these businesses is that sooner or later they will disappear. Their poor working conditions turn away younger people, and they can't afford to invest in new infrastructure or train new craftsmen. But if the government regards the technologies, skills, and potential of SUMs as resources, and invests in and develops them, they can fulfill their huge potential."

In 2013, Ms. Chun led Korea's trade minister and several lawmakers on a tour of garment factories and other areas surrounding Dongdaemun Market. Afterward, the tour participants were unanimous in saying: "We must revitalize these industries. Neglecting them for so long makes no sense."

Says Ms. Chun: "Frankly, until now, when we thought of manufacturers, we only thought about large businesses like automakers, shipbuilders, and heavy industry. People said that traditional manufacturing that relies on manual labor was obsolete, or fading away. In the late 1980s, Korea's manufacturing sector was pretty lackluster. That was not the case in the U.S. and Germany, however. New York City, a world fashion capital, rolled out policies to help fashion-focused manufacturers prosper, while in Germany, even small-scale pencil makers have secure footing."

# Even Samsung and SK made money from clothes

—

When you look at the clothing and sewing industry, Korea is categorized as a developed country. We are ahead of Peru, Cambodia, and Vietnam, but behind Italy, France, and the U.S. The countries that are behind us have cheap labor but lack technological know-how. Those ahead of us have influential global brands thanks to outstanding technology and designs, but they lack production lines. In contrast, we possess both. By restoring local production lines, we can offer prices that compete with other overseas manufacturing hubs and also deliver outstanding design and technological expertise. And in terms of the sheer number of small-scale factories, almost no country can compare with Korea.

Japan, which was the world's largest textile exporter as recently as the 1970s, when the industry entered a steady decline, envies us. But Korean policy makers were the only ones ignorant of the fact that Korea is blessed with so many advantages.

"If we keep neglecting these businesses, we will never produce decent brands like the developed countries did, and our outstanding technological abilities will fade away. We need to build national brands. Once we succeed in helping a mid-sized company create a global brand, it will only be a matter of time before we turn it into a global enterprise."

At this point, Ms. Chun pauses to reflect on the history of the textile industry.

"How did the big conglomerates make money in the early days? By making clothing. It was true for Sunkyoung, Cheil, LG, and Samsung. With the money they earned, they carved a path into industries such as shipbuilding, electronics, IT, heavy industry, and construction. What did they do next? Big businesses that grew on the back of their clothing lines let their own apparel brands die. Nowadays, they pay royalties to import clothing to sell in department stores."

She says she cannot understand why they do that.

"If I were the head of a conglomerate, I would chart out a 10-year strategy and investment plan to create a top brand. If they had kept investing, within three or four decades they would have had at least one global brand. But they abandoned the businesses that fueled their early growth, and sent the people who were working in those businesses out into the streets."

Nonetheless, she insists that SUMs have not entirely given up on themselves.

"Do you know what it means that small factories never shut down? These days, mom-and-pop businesses usually call it quits within three years. In contrast, the average SUM stays in business for over a decade. Why don't they shut down so easily? Staying open means they can make ends meet and send their children to school. In short, their businesses make money and have the potential to grow!

Indeed, the clothing and sewing industry will never fade away. We say, 'clothing, food, and shelter.' Is there anyone who does not wear clothing? Though they may involve backbreaking labor and aren't big money-makers, these businesses stay afloat. That's what matters!"

*"If they had kept investing, within three or four decades
they would have had at least one global brand. But they abandoned
the businesses that fueled their early growth, and sent the people
who were working in those businesses out into the streets."*

# Back to Dongdaemun

—

In 1989, Ms. Chun moved to the U.K. to study labor sociology. After earning her doctorate for her thesis, "They Are Not Machines," she came back to Korea in 2001. She returned to Dongdaemun, where she became a "well-educated assistant sewing machine operator." While working for six months at three sewing shops employing eight or nine workers each, she realized two things: One, nothing is changing in this field; and two, I can at least make ends meet since I have the skills to do so.

"I wondered whether it was the same story in other shops, so starting in June 2003 I visited and surveyed all 500 sewing factories in Changshin-dong. Most of them were 10- or 20-year-old shops that stayed open regardless of how much business they had. Since the factory owners were also technicians, they wouldn't close up shop even if they were forced to lay off workers. Most of the sewing machine operators at these factories were in their 40s or 50s and were grateful for their skills. They would say that, were it not for their skills, they would have to work with Korean-Chinese migrants in simple restaurants, which would be hard at their age. So I started thinking about how I could make them happier in their workplace..."

Over the next 11 years, she did a great deal of work. In 2003, she founded Chamteo, a non-profit group dedicated to women's welfare and labor. Three years later, she founded the Korean Fashion Sewing Academy, which helped garment workers improve their skills to produce high value-added products. Then, together with 20 academy graduates, she started a social enterprise called Chaamot.

"When I was studying labor relations in Britain, I learned about Robert

Owen (1771–1858) who became known as the "father of co-operatives."
During the Industrial Revolution, a lot of spinning mills sprang up in the U.K.
and Scotland, where machines would make yarn from sheep wool. If too much
sheep's wool dust built up, the machines would get stuck, so someone had to
clean away the dust. That job was done by four-or five-year-old children who,
thanks to their small size, could easily crawl under the machines and wipe the
dust. Seeking to address such workplace realities, Owen developed an ideal
workers community by the standards of that time. In this community, people
worked for eight hours a day, got three meals a day, and were assured a certain
salary. Five teachers were hired to teach the kids. He was trying to provide the
basics for the community."

She goes on to say that she was surprised by what she discovered while
reading about Robert Owen: His ideal community was quite similar to the "ideal
enterprise" described in *The Biography of Chun Tae-il.*

"The model enterprise that my elder brother envisioned was a factory,
established with KRW 30 million in capital, equipped with 50 sewing
machines, and employing 157 workers. He also planned to hire five teachers.
Back then, a lot of workers could not complete elementary school. He added
the condition that the teachers would be paid less than the machine operators
because, he said, operating a sewing machine and making clothing amounts
to both physical and intellectual labor, while teachers only need to expend
intellectual labor. He couldn't have been aware of Owen or read his book. So
how could he come up with the same idea?"

Mimicking her brother's "model enterprise," she launched Chaamot, a
sewing enterprise that operates under the principle of eight hours of work per
day, guaranteed days off, and coverage in the four main types of insurance. Ms.
Chun says that although the company set an example among sewing businesses

and its name meant a "really fun workplace," her four years of managing the business were anything but fun.

"For our first three years, we focused on ramping up our skills to make the best quality clothing regardless of what kinds of clothes were ordered. As time went by, we built up a good reputation, namely, for being a bit pricey but offering quality goods. It was like, when they first came to us, they would find us too expensive and go to other manufacturers, but eventually they came back. In that sense, I suppose the company is on solid footing."

That experience made her acutely aware of how hard it is to run a manufacturing business, and gave her a deeper understanding of the pain and suffering endured at SUMs. Due to the nature of their work, SUMs cannot relocate, even as land prices are pushed up by new apartment complexes and urban development. But their landlords are so eager to evict them... and they're driven out of the cities. Given these realities, she pondered over how to invigorate, sustain, and develop their businesses. So it's fair to say that she already had the concept of the Act in mind when she first set foot in the National Assembly.

## Encountering pearls in the mud
—

The nine artisans featured in this book are people she met during her eleven years around Changsin-dong and three years in the National Assembly. Among them, Ms. Chun had a special relationship with three sewing artisans in particular.

"I first met Ms. Kim Do-yeong in February of 2009, some months after I started Chaamot. One day I went to work, and saw a woman roaming around the building entrance. I asked her why she was there. She said she had seen a newspaper article about me and wanted to talk to me. She had operated a sewing machine her entire life, but now she wanted to change her job. She wanted to be an instructor at the sewing academy, working for the social enterprise. I told her, 'That's a very good idea but you need to get training at the academy before you can become an instructor and work here.' She actually completed the academy, worked as an assistant instructor for almost a year, and then came to work for Chammot. Later on, she was promoted to an instructor, and then set up and began running a workshop. These days, she always says that finding out about the sewing academy changed her life. She takes pride in and enjoys her work and teaching."

Ms. Chun met Mr. Han Sang-min, a master tailor featured in Chapter 3, through the sewing academy as well.

"When I first set up the academy in 2006, most of the instructors were professors from colleges or universities. But after a semester, I found that it wasn't working. The trainees were coming to the academy to improve their skills, but they already had 10 to 20 years of experience. A trainer who was not an expert in the field could not teach them. So I went to Jangan-dong, an area known for its many quasi-fashion factories, and told them that I was looking for a highly skilled technician to be an instructor. They introduced me to Mr. Han. He was so unsophisticated that, standing before the students, his cheeks would turn red and he couldn't even utter his own name. But he insisted that though he was pretty lousy at explaining things in words, he could teach — and was willing to. He had such outstanding skills; the trainees really liked him."

Jang Hyo-ung, the director of the sewing academy, also came to meet her after reading her interview in the paper. Teary-eyed and audibly angry, he

*That experience made her acutely aware of how hard it is to run a manufacturing business, and pondered over how to invigorate, sustain, and develop their businesses. So it's fair to say that she already had the concept of the Act in mind when she first set foot in the National Assembly.*

shared long, pent-up stories about how technicians like him worked so hard, honed their skills, and contributed to Korea's economic growth but were still ignored by society. After the meeting, Mr. Jang, a clothes pattern technician earning a six-figure salary, started teaching at the academy. He continued doing so for eight years and, after retiring from his company, took over as director of the academy.

She discovered many other hidden pearls besides these three, and decided to proudly present them to the world. On December 2, 2006, she held the 1st Suda Gongbang Fashion Show.

"I told them to take the stage in clothing they had made themselves. But they'd rather not, they said, because whenever I do something, it ends up all over the newspapers and then the world will know that they are sewing machine operators. Most of them kept their job secret from their daughters' boyfriends and their in-laws and the like. Some of them even told me not to use them to build my reputation."

But Ms. Chun was not easily discouraged. She joined a two-day workshop with academy trainees. The original plan was to go to Goesan, North Chunchcheong province, but on account of rainstorms, they went to a *jjimjilbang* (Korean-style sauna) in Ilsan Instead. There, Ms. Chun talked about an article she had read about a pink-ribbon fashion show whose models were breast cancer patients, and went to great lengths to persuade the trainees to change their minds.

"I said, 'Imagine how hard it would have been for women who had had their breasts removed to go onstage. But they worked up the courage to tell the world that, even without breasts, they are still women and still themselves. You also need to break the wall and come out. Be proud of yourself. You have skills. Thanks to those skills, you could send your kids to school, and they could meet a good spouse, and you have such well-to-do in-laws. So will you live the rest of your life ashamed of your job? Tell all of them how proud you are of your skills.'"

Eventually they were won over, and the fashion show was a resounding success. There was such a large turnout — the crowd numbered over 2,000 — that the hall could not accommodate everyone. After the show, the stage was awash in the tears of the trainees, all of them middle-aged women, who recalled it as being the first time in their lives to receive a bouquet of flowers from their husband and children. They smiled and wept, and wept and smiled. Armed with newfound confidence and brimming with motivation after the show, they said they would love to join more fashion shows, bringing their daughters onstage with them the next time.

The second confidence-building program that Ms. Chun arranged was "resume writing." Many of the first graduates of the academy went on to become instructors. In December 2009, she organized a three-day workshop for them on Jeju Island.

"Frankly, they have been lying about their backgrounds. They say they graduated from middle school or high school. By saying that, their number of years of work experience would be shortened by three to six years. So I told them to be honest and write down everything: Describe in detail when they began working at a factory, how many years they worked as an assistant sewing machine operator, as a main operator, and whether they produced children's wear or ladies suits. I told them, 'You see how well-educated people have a detailed resume? People see it and recognize their work. But you just vaguely say something like 10 years here, 20 years there. So no one believes it. So they do not recognize your work experience, and try to push down your salary during negotiations. Prove your skills and your life through your resume.'"

She says that despite her persuasive efforts, they continued to lie. She thought they would never change. But change finally came around 2011. To attract trainees, the academy held three rounds of information sessions like those held by Gangnam cram schools, drawing over 100 people each time. Before the sessions, she encouraged instructors to show off their work in their subject areas.

"I still can't forget the day. I sat in the back row as the instructors introduced themselves one by one. Then Mr. Han Sang-min, who was always bashful, told them, 'I only completed elementary school. I began working at a tailor shop in Gwangju and stayed in that field for three decades.' Listening to his story had me in tears. They were accepting who they were. It felt as if a floodgate had opened. The other teachers who had been continually lying also started to reveal themselves. Watching them being proud of themselves made me happy, but it was heart-wrenching and sad at the same time..."

Of course, technicians don't have to prove themselves through academic achievements. For them, what they make and how well they make it are the be-all and end-all, and enough for them to feel acknowledged. Even so, Ms. Chun wanted them to embrace and take pride in not only the skills that had carried them through their life but their entire life story. This book contains the stories of people who underwent such a process and gathered the strength to tell the world: "I am an artisan."

## My entire identity comes from my brother, But I will not give up my ways

—

Ms. Chun is considered a diligent legislator not only in the TIEC but also within the entire National Assembly. She has sponsored 68 bills tackling issues that range from labor, human rights and industry, to public enterprises and public welfare. Among them, the Act is at the heart of her legislative activities. Indeed, she was honored as an Outstanding Lawmaker in 2014 based on her legislative activity and policy development, and bestowed with Korea's Best Legislation Award from *Money Today* magazine in recognition of the value of the Act. Since a lawmaker is in effect a legislative body, that amounted to Ms. Chun recognized as the best lawmaker. After more than 10 years in her field, she had already sensed how inaccessible the law appeared to be. So at first, she hesitated to become a lawmaker when the job was offered to her. But people urged her on, saying: "Go to the National Assembly; you can accomplish many things there."

"I suppose if a lawmaker has the will, they can do a lot of things. I've realized how important it is to enact laws. Without laws, the central or local government may not do what they want. But once a law is passed, it must be adhered to. It seems that if a politician wants to change the world with some ideas or philosophy, they can change the important part, though not all of it. I am amazed seeing how important it is to be able to do these kinds of things."

Immediately after she became a lawmaker, the Korean Fashion Industry Green Forum was established at the National Assembly, which she co-chaired together with lawmaker Chung Sye-kyun. That's where the Act was conceived.

She and researchers from the Institute of Legal Studies and the Korea Federation of Small and Medium Business put their heads together, focusing on formulating the new concept, "small urban manufacturers." Even though small-scale merchants and manufacturers were collectively referred to as a "small commercial and industrial business," only the former, such as those in traditional markets and general sole proprietors, were beneficiaries of policies, and few policies existed to help SUMs. Through in-depth research, surveys and relentless persuasion, she succeeded in dividing small enterprises into two categories — small merchants and SUMs — for conceptual and administrative purposes. From there, she spearheaded the establishment of the Small Urban Manufacturers Office within the Small and Medium Business Administration.

Striving to get the bill enacted, she appealed to as many lawmakers as possible, regardless of party, by explaining the importance and intent of the bill, and invited them on field trips to enlist their sympathy with her cause. She believed it had to be done to deliver greater benefits to people. In addition, even after a bill is passed, it must be implemented through cooperation from different ministries. Here, her reputation as a "balanced" lawmaker to her colleagues in both the ruling and opposition parties helped her.

"Given my background, many people assume I have hard-line views and an uncompromising style or that I'm hard to talk to. But once they meet me, they change their minds. Isn't that nice?"

Some complain that she has betrayed the country's labor force. They believed she would join the Environment and Labor Committee (the "ELC") after becoming a lawmaker.

"I know there are some who are disappointed. I also know that there are people who want me to join the ELC, battle over workers' rights, and march out front at labor strikes. But I have my way. That does not mean I would avoid the labor community. I want to focus on 'solving fundamental problems.' I think grappling with the problems that are bubbling over the surface won't work. We need to identify and address the root causes of those problems. It takes longer, but it's important. In order to do that, I've soldiered on quietly."

She says she won't conform to existing frameworks. If she fits herself into the framework defined by others, one which dictates how she should live or speak,

*"It seems that if a politician wants to change the world with some ideas or philosophy, they can change the important part, though not all of it. I am amazed to see how important it is to be able to do these kinds of things."*

it would be impossible to come up with fresh ideas, she says. Nonetheless, she credits her brother Chun Tae-il as the source of all of her ideas.

"My whole background is my brother. That doesn't change no matter how long ago the incident occurred. I have not lived a life like that of my brother or my mom. But it is clear that they are the underlying reasons why I think the way I think or do what I am doing. It's just that our methods are a little different. And that's because, over time, the environment has changed."

She's confident that, for SUMs that have worked quietly in the background until now, the Act will offer a fresh starting point for transforming their dreams into reality.

"Martin Luther King, Jr. said he had a dream. He wanted to see the day when it doesn't matter how poor you are, or what color of skin you have, and a day when black and white eat at the same table. And he realized his dream. I, too, want to make my dream come true."

Her dream is to see the day when you can find people wearing Korean brand clothes anywhere in the world; when bags, shoes, and jewelry made in Korea are considered the best products in the world; and when the artisans and technicians who make those products can work happily and with pride! To realize that dream, her brother ignited the fire, her mother tilled the earth, and she is about to make the flowers blossom. The history of labor written by a family is now unfolding in Dongdaemun, and is about to bring another scene change to Korea.

*Who says
manufacturing is
a sunset industry?*

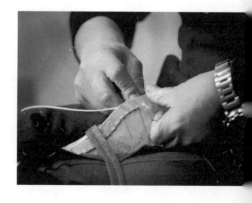

"As my breath and the movements of the sewing machine become one,
I feel completely at peace."
Kim Do-yeong (Expert Seamstress, 43 years of work)

I Would Not Trade This Honest Work of Shoemaking for a Harvard Degree
Yu Hong-shik (Master Shoemaker, 55 years of work)

Happy Craftspeople Make Masterpieces
Kim Jong-eun  (Master Bag Maker, 42 years of work)

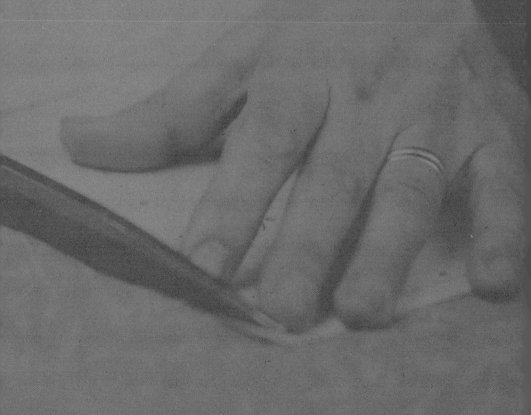

# CHAPTER 1

—

# Crafts never betray you

# Kim
# Do-yeong

—

Expert Seamstress,
43 years of work

"As my breath and the movements of
the sewing machine become one,
I feel completely at peace."

—

| | |
|---|---|
| 1959 | Born in Busan. Moved to Seoul at age three. |
| 1973 | Began working, at age 14, as a seamstress' assistant at a dressmaking factory in Donghwa Market. |
| 1978 | Began working as a seamstress. |
| 1999 | Passed the middleschool diploma examination at age 40. |
| 2011 | Began teaching classes at the Korea Academy of Fashion and Sewing. Opened her own workshop. |
| Present | Continues to teach dressmaking at the Academy while running her own workshop. |

# A Small Workspace above Ground

—

Spring was just around the corner. Perhaps that is why that day in February felt especially chilly. I got off the subway at the Shinseol-dong Station and began to walk along a narrow alleyway. Small shops of similar sizes were lined up along the road. Indifference — or was it a lack of wariness against the outside world? — was the dominant mood in this alleyway. The few locals who were out on the street looked as natural a part of the landscape as the fences and the shops.

This alleyway, with its ambience still trapped in the 1980s, is, along with Changshin-dong, a place replete with memories of the tumults of modern Korea. The cradle of apparel and dressmaking industries of Korea, Shinseol-dong, along with the Pyeonghwa Market, is a source of the enduring legacy that has sustained the evolving and thriving Dongdaemun fashion market to this day. The long and winding alleyway gently hummed with the sounds of diligent sewing machines. The countless new garments created in this neighborhood are shipped to locations both in and outside Korea on a daily basis.

I was on my way to the workshop of Kim Do-yeong, an expert seamstress who had worked in this neighborhood for 43 years on end. I could not begin to fathom the depth of experience Kim must have, working tirelessly in front of her sewing machine for more than four decades and witnessing all the vicissitudes of the outside world at the same time.

Kim's workshop was located on the second floor of a small building. The inside of the workshop was filled with cutting boards, sewing machines, racks loaded with fabrics of all kinds. Kim kept apologizing for making me travel all the way to such a humble place, when an interview could have been better held at a café, presumably with a nicer atmosphere. Little did she know how much awe I felt as I began to climb up the narrow staircase with her. Before I came to this place, I assumed that her workshop would be underground, like the vast majority of other dressmaking factories. How refreshing it was for me to see a seamstress working above ground! The workspace was brightly lit and by far in one of the best conditions I had seen in dressmaking workshops.

The only minor complaint I had was how cold it felt inside the workshop. The building it was in was old and lacked a central heating system. Kim had worked in this workshop without any heating device until last winter or so, but decided to bring in a small gasoline heater this year. Yet I became worried for her because the room was not warm enough for anyone to work.

Kim brought me a cup of coffee, and immediately returned to her standing position by her cutting board, saying she needed to hurry to finish her work. I sat somewhere nearby that cutting board, taking care not to bother her while working, but also to observe her as up close as possible. The expert seamstress began to cut away at her fabric along the pattern. The repetitive sound of her well-tamed scissors, attesting to her mastery over her craft, was quite comforting.

## "I am skilled at what I do. There will be no retirement for me."

——

**Do you always have so much work to do?**

No, winter tends to be less busy for me, from December to February. I do get orders for tailoring from time to time, so I can take few days off from work even during winter anyway. The one I am working on right now is a padded coat for a woman. I am making it by filling natural-dyed fabric with cotton.

**You are in your mid-50s now, so how could you have worked at this for 43 years?**

I began working in this line of work right after I finished sixth grade. Back then, it was common for housewives to gather around and boast about how much their daughters earned by working in factories. Every time I eavesdropped on such a conversation, I kept thinking that I should find work as soon as I finished elementary school. It was common for women my age to find work after finishing sixth grade back then.

**Where did you find your first job?**

I began to work as a *shida* (assistant) at a dressmaking workshop at the Donghwa Market, nearby the Pyeonghwa Market. My job, like that of all other *shidas*, was to do all the prep work so that seamstresses could work using their sewing machines. It took years for *shidas* to have their work recognized and be able to begin using sewing machines. In our world, we used to say 'one rode a sewing machine' when we talked about how one finally graduated from one's *shida*-hood and began working as a seamstress.

**It must have taken a lot of hard work until you were able to finally "ride a sewing machine."**

Seamstresses were not so willing to impart their knowledge and skills to *shidas*. We novices did everything we could to learn their art, fighting to sit before a sewing machine during the lunch hour and doing everything to please the seamstresses. It was never easy to have these seamstresses finally say "yes" to our pleas. I worked as a *shida* for several years myself. The work itself was not that hard, compared to the kind of psychological bullying and anxiety I was put through.

**Is it still like that today in this industry?**

No way! We can hardly find even a few who are interested in learning this craft. We would be so delighted to teach and train any who came to our doors looking for work. Our case was different. Anyone was willing to work almost for free — for a bit of food — at the time. Looking back, I think I did well by learning this craft through doing the *shida* work. I have worked so hard, and am not afraid of working hard any more. Seamstresses today learn how to work sewing machines first without doing any apprentice work, so they have difficulty doing other, yet related, work. People like me, on the other hand, can do almost anything and achieve both quality and speed.

**You sound quite proud of your work.**

In the past, I was afraid of telling people that I worked as a seamstress. It was a lowly job, someone others would always look down upon. To be called a "factory girl" was traumatizing enough for me. People who worked in manual factories and in publishing were easily looked down upon at the time. We were never treated right for what we did. Now, though, all my friends are envious of me for having my own career and working at this late an age. Dressmaking is something I could do all my life, as long as I stay healthy. I am grateful and proud now that I have mastered this craft.

**It's good that you are taking pride in your work. But hasn't it cost you anything?**

The only thing I regret is that I did not have enough education. Back when I started working in this field, when I was so little, my plan was to work for only a few years and save enough money so that I could return to school. That plan never came through because I was so busy working for many years. Some of my coworkers my age had enough sense to enroll in night schools and classes. I could not dream of that. The factory owners hated workers studying and

The expert seamstress began to cut away
at her fabric along the pattern.
The repetitive sound of her well-tamed scissors, attesting
to her mastery over her craft, was quite comforting.

threatened to kick them out, saying such workers would 'contaminate' the atmosphere. So I gave up on my dream of learning and immersed myself in work. As the years went on, though, I came to regret my choice all the more.

**When did you decide to change?**

When I turned 40! So I took the middle school diploma examination. I think I did well to get a middle school diploma then. I thought, if I did not do it, I would not die and rest peacefully because of the lingering regret.

Kim still thinks that she needs to study and learn. She spends the vast majority of her time working with a sewing machine, and cannot easily find time to study. Yet she keeps telling herself that she will return to studying someday. Her wish is to write something beautiful after learning and studying more.


# "Price competition forces even skilled technicians out of the market."

———

Kim is one of the most skilled and experienced seamstresses in the dressmaking industry. Yet dressmaking businesses in Korea constantly complain of the dearth of skilled and reliable seamstresses and tailors. Why is there so little supply when there is so much demand?

To this question, Kim answered: "We acknowledge that there are numerous people in this industry who work as quickly as possible, focusing on quantity rather than quality. But the system itself also encourages that. Our clients demand good quality, yet also keep trying to lower the cost. I get a lot of fashion designers who visit me here. They talk this and that about their ideas and visions, but end up going to seamstresses who offer better prices. Being quality-minded means having to spend that much more time. Quality tailor-made clothes cannot be made without putting in the effort and time. Few people are willing to accept this truth today. Given the work we put into dressmaking, we should probably get at least half the prices being paid for the clothes we make. I do not understand why fashion designers try to cut costs on our end only.

**How much are you getting paid for the jacket you are making now?**

I'm getting paid about KRW 100,000. I have to cut three different types of fabric for this jacket alone, including the upper, the cotton, and the lining. I don't think KRW 100,000 is expensive for this kind of work. But I know there are inexperienced part-time seamstresses who are paid much less. These seamstresses are paid by the number of clothes they make each day, so they are forced to work like machines. I do not understand how they can get by on such low fees. They get about KRW 8,000 to KRW 10,000 for a woman's jacket and KRW 20,000 for a man's winter coat. This is simply unacceptable. During idle seasons, there are countless people who are willing to work for even less. We who work in the same industry should unite together and set the price floors, below which we agree not to work. But this unionization is far easier said than done. A few seamstresses may decide to unionize like that, but there will always be other seamstresses willing to work for lower fees.

**There may be few expert seamstresses, but there are many seamstresses.**

That's right. This dressmaking industry must be something. A great number of people working in areas like Changshin-dong, Shindang-dong, and Miari work in this industry. They raise their families on the money they earn by working in their jobs for years and decades. This industry is still alive and thriving.

**The number of foreign workers in the Korean manufacturing sector is on the rise. How about the dressmaking industry?**

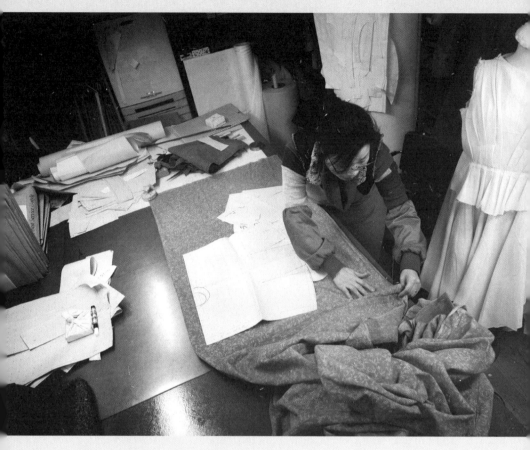

"This dressmaking industry must be something.
A great number of people working in areas
like Changshin-dong, Shindang-dong, and Miari work in this industry.
They raise their families on the money they earn by working
in their jobs for years and decades.
This industry is still alive and thriving."

We have the same phenomenon in this field, too. We have great demand for skilled hands, but few Koreans are willing to learn and work in this trade. When I receive an order for 100 clothes or so, I seek help from hired hands. These are mostly Vietnamese women. They are quite skilled at what they do, and have a keen eye for what is demanded. They mostly have day jobs somewhere else, where they work during the week, and work on my orders on the weekends. They are hardworking and talented. They plan to go back to their country for the upcoming New Year's holidays. I wouldn't know what to do without them.

**It must be difficult to find new Koreans in this field these days.**

More and more dressmaking factories are avoiding hiring fellow Koreans, as Koreans demand higher fees and can be picky to work with. Fast fashion stores like H&M today offer wide selections of cheap and pretty clothes. All these clothes are cut and sewn somewhere in the Third World. My Korean colleagues and I cannot begin to imagine how we could produce such clothes at such low prices. The dressmaking industry in Korea faces steep competition from these global chains, and our future remains murky.

Kim sat in front of her sewing machine with cotton-lined pieces of fabric. She had finished cutting the fabric and now needed to sew. She changed hands and the fabric pieces a few times, and the sewing machine began to roll.

## "Cross the bridge of despair to see hope."

—

"Sometimes, I become intoxicated with the sound of the sewing machine motor rolling. I may feel down, tired, or angry, but listening to this sound of the sewing machine for hours never fails to calm me down. My heart is filled with peace whenever I work with my sewing machine. I had a brief stint as an insurance saleswoman. I envied people working in insurance, so quit the seamstress job to convert. After a while, though, I realized that I wasn't cut out for insurance. I just never felt at peace while working in sales. When I sewed, all I cared about was how many clothes I could make a day. Insurance was a completely different world."

**Now you teach and train students. Isn't that also a fancy job?**

I cannot stand sitting around. Every winter, I receive fewer orders than in other seasons, so I have to find some work to fill my time. I have worked as a seamstress as long as I can remember, but always felt looked down upon, frustrated that my devotion and craft are not receiving due recognition. About six years ago, I came across a newspaper article about the Korean Advanced Sewing Skills Academy (KASSA). I went straight to the workshop at the Real Women Welfare Center in Jangchung-dong after reading the article, and sat down with you [*Chun Soon-ok, the interviewer*]. You worked as the head director of the center at the time before you became a National Assemblywoman. I remember telling you: "I want to work with you, too. Please tell me what I can do."

**I remember that day vividly, too.**

As I was talking with you, I realized that we shared so much in common in terms of aspirations and dreams. That conversation with you gave me hope that I could finally do something meaningful with the skills I have learned over the decades.

**Yes, I remember suggesting that you teach dressmaking at the Academy.**

That's right. You also advised that I complete the instructor training program first, since dressmaking was one thing and teaching, another. Taking your advice, I learned the theories and techniques of teaching for six months, and have been teaching at the Academy for five years in a row. Each semester, I go there to teach two or three classes a week. These days, when I am on break from the Academy, I also teach dressmaking classes at Didimteo, a center for immigrant women.

**How does it feel now that you have become a teacher?**

It gives me a new sense of fulfillment. Some of my students even went to college, but still come to my classes to learn dressmaking. When I see them, I feel a newfound appreciation for the trade I have learned and practiced for so many years.

**How old are your students? Does your class help them find the jobs they want?**

Most of my students are in their 30s and 40s. Dressmaking as a trade is indifferent to age. Once you have learned the necessary techniques and skills, you can easily find a job. But staying long in your job is another matter. Well-skilled seamstresses can earn steady income, but I find a lot more non-Koreans working in this field today than Koreans. My students take my classes because they want to find jobs as seamstresses, but they tend to quit their jobs after a while because they find the pay and the working conditions unbearable. In my classes, I keep telling them to persevere, but perseverance is not so appreciated as a virtue these days.

**Do you feel sorry for your well-trained students who cannot apply their newly learned art?**

I cannot describe how sorry and disheartened I feel. People today think of a craft as something they could study and learn. In order for a craft to become my own, however, I must work in the same field for many years. People today have difficulty bearing with this process, and they let their skills and talents go to waste.

**Would you say your students need to become more realistic about the world?**

Our job is to deliver our orders on time. When orders and workloads pile up, we sometimes have to stay up past midnight to finish the given day's work. There are schedules and timetables when you are self-employed. Our job is to help our clients meet these deadlines on time. But not everyone knows what to expect when they enter this line of work. Aspiring seamstresses learn their craft and look for jobs, hoping they can land one that will allow them to go home at six o'clock sharp. But that is simply not how manufacturing works in Korea. Sometimes, I run into students who have no idea about — and have little willingness to bear with — the real working conditions in this field. I wonder where they learned otherwise.

**Nevertheless, should we not try to improve working conditions for seamstresses?**

Of course we should. Once the conditions at our worksites are improved, we may be able to attract younger and better-educated generations. And we should try harder to afford our workers more humane treatment. Things have improved much in the field, but newcomers may still find it hard to adapt to their jobs.

**I was delighted to discover that your workshop is located on the second floor of a building. Few dressmaking workshops are found above ground.**

I can tell fellow seamstresses from a mile away. Because we tend to work for many hours, sitting in the same spot without ever seeing daylight, we have this fatigued, lackluster air about us, similar to withered plants. I kept a workshop underground for about two years, and it hurt my health. I never want to make the same mistake again.

"Every winter, I receive fewer orders than in other seasons,
so I have to find some work to fill my time.
I have worked as a seamstress as long
as I can remember, but always felt looked down upon, frustrated that
my devotion and craft are not receiving due recognition"

# "I take pride in the quality of the clothes I make, not in how quickly I can make them."

——

Kim's hands kept moving about busily at an astonishing pace. One moment she had started backstitches, the next a finished piece of clothing was hanging from the cutting board. I gently dragged the bottom part of the backstitched fabric down below the workstation so that it would not bother our seamstress as she kept working on other parts. This brought back memories of my own days working as a *shida*. Kim smiled at me.

"You know, back then, we all had to work with our knees on the floor. The work was brutal on our knees. The sewing machine stations back then were not as high as this one today, so countless *shidas* had to kneel down."

Kim slowed down, trying to organize her thoughts before she spoke further.

"Back then, when I didn't know much about this craft, I thought speed was everything. Now I know enough to make every second I spend here count for the quality of my clothes."

**Are you saying you are not working as quickly as you could? You seem to be working at a lightning speed already to me.**

Are you kidding me? At this speed, I can say I am almost killing time! I guess you have not been to factories where dozens of part-time seamstresses work. Those factories are unbelievably busy. Go to the male apparel section, and you will see pairs of seamstresses and *shidas* working side by side, as if forming a human conveyor belt. In our times, seamstresses earned far more than *shidas*. These days, they share their fees in equal parts. Today's *shidas* know all the techniques and skills so that seamstresses can focus solely on stitching work. The world is not what it used to be. We could not dare look seamstresses in the eye in the past. Their words were law to us. No seamstress has that much authority today.

**How do you solve conflicts you have with designers? Fashion designers and seamstresses are bound to work together, and quarrel a lot, in making clothing.**

Sometimes, I get fashion designers who come to me with designs that have no room for sewing. Dressmaking is about mastering the creation of silhouettes, and we cannot sew a piece of clothing exactly according to the design. So we may suggest that a few minor changes to the design may be necessary. Some designers take offense at this suggestion, thinking we do not respect their vision and work.

**Some fashion designers say that they cannot create new styles and designs because of the limited abilities and skills of the seamstresses.**

Seamstresses may also be at fault to an extent. Some seamstresses really think of everything in terms of money, demanding this much for a sample, and that much for extra needlework. They also try to avoid work that is not likely to turn significant profit. As someone involved in the same trade, I feel ashamed of these attitudes. Dressmaking is not just a means to making money. It is a source of pride and the meaning of life. Dressmakers working in high fashion are a little different in this regard. I see many of them working with a sense of vocation. Both designers and seamstresses need to acknowledge their faults and try to make improvements together, making and accepting necessary concessions. But there are also teams of designers and seamstresses who get along very well.

**I cannot help but detect a note of sadness in what you have just said.**

Some of the fashion designers I encounter do so little work that I have difficulty distinguishing between them and *shidas* of my younger days. Yet some fashion designers are so arrogant that they look down on us seamstresses. They seem to forget that, no matter how beautiful the patterns and designs are, the quality of the resulting product depends as much on our skills and dedication as on their designs.

# "Now I know the true value of my work."

—

Interviewing Kim, I could not help but wonder how many more such skilled and experienced seamstresses there may be in Korea. I hoped that more seamstresses like Kim would come out into the world, share their knowledge and techniques, and gather their ideas together to create a better working environment for the next generations of dressmakers.

"There are indeed many dressmakers with amazing skills and expertise. Put them next to machines, and you would not be able to tell which is which. Just think of how much time and effort they must have put into mastering their craft. In their youth, they probably made hundreds, even thousands, of clothes each day. Working like a machine means that your body reacts to, and handles, your given task before your head does. When you do that, you are a master of your art. I am confident that seamstresses of my generation can compete with seamstresses elsewhere and even machines. They also know how to work new machines. It is difficult today to find craftspeople with such comprehensive knowledge of their art."

**What do you think of the fact that so many of these skilled craftspeople disappear into oblivion?**

It is a gloomy reality we face. They can do so much good for the world by imparting their knowledge. I wish they knew the social meaning of their skills. But many of these master craftspeople lack the time or the peace of mind to look around and see things other than the given tasks. Factories in Changshin-dong are filled with expert dressmakers, but few of them have ever heard of the Korean Advanced Sewing Skills Academy(KASSA). They are so immersed in their work that they take little interest in the outside world.

**Aren't you a rarity in your field, then?**

I think so. My colleagues used to treat me as an oddball, as someone who made life more difficult by exploring and expecting more. My colleagues spent their leisure time working, making a few more T-shirts. I, on the other hand, kept traveling about in search of new things to learn. I could not tell them that there must be better ways of living than this. They just would not understand. I think it is about different values. Some people value making as much money as possible by spending all their time on moneymaking activities. I value something else.

**Is it really all about personal value differences?**

No, it is not. Our society refuses to recognize people who have mastered their trades and crafts. Distributors in the apparel industry, for example, ask us what good it would be to make clothes if there were no channels of distribution. They ask such a question because they can only think from their own perspective, without regard for people who make things with their hands. Few are interested in how hard we work, and how bad the working conditions are. We have learned this craft to avoid hunger, and we still hold this job almost exclusively as a means to make money. So, what other meaning can we find in our work, and whom can we teach?

As Kim's hands moved about, a finished jacket appeared before my eyes as if

"Back then, when I didn't know much about this craft,
I thought speed was everything.
Now I know enough to make every second
I spend here count for the quality of my clothes."

out of a dream. I gasped in wonder and awe, and told Kim that I admired with what ease she created such a perfect piece of clothing.

"All this may appear easy to you and others," Kim answered, "but there is nothing so easy in this world. I make this look easy because I have been doing the same work for so long. Now I am taking a class on pattern-making. It's really fun. If I have spare time, I would also like to learn about fashion design."

Kim comes to work at 9 o'clock in the morning and leaves at 11 o'clock at night to take the day's last bus home. She still dreams of mastering her craft and other related arts and achieve something that she can call wholly her own. That is because she has realized that she is not just a seamstress, and that sewing does a lot more for the world than she thought.

How can we demean anyone who works steadfastly and tirelessly with her own hands in order to earn a living for herself and her family? The world is a cold place that constantly forces us to think of ourselves as less than we really are and as less than others, even though the hard work we do entitles us to dignity. Kim's endeavors are noteworthy because they have helped her reclaim her value and dignity in the world despite its disdain. The value Kim views in her work as she expounded in her soothing yet confident voice still echoes in my heart.

Yu
Hong-shik

—

Master Shoemaker
55 years of work

# I Would Not Trade This Honest Work of Shoemaking for a Harvard Degree

—

| | |
|---|---|
| 1949 | Born in Gwangju, Jeollanam-do. |
| 1961 | Began to learn the craft of handmade shoes at Gineung Jehwa in Seoul, at age 13. |
| 1967 | Began to teach others shoemaking at age 19. |
| 1979 | Returned to Gwangju and opened his own handmade shoes shop. |
| 1997 | Returned to Seoul and began to walk the path of a master shoemaker. |
| 2006 | Founded Dream Jehwa. |
| 2013 | Officially named Seoul's first "Master Shoemaker." |
| Present | Continues to run Dream Jehwa and teach future generations of shoemakers. |

Have you ever seen a master shoemaker make and complete a pair of shoes right before your eyes? If you are interested, I suggest that you visit Seongsu-dong, Seoul, where you can meet a shoemaker who has honed and perfected his craft over 55 years.

The district of Seongdong-gu houses over 500 shoemaking and related businesses (including 300 or so shoemakers around the Seongsu Subway Station), and over 100 businesses supplying shoe materials and distributing finished shoes. Taking pride in its history and tradition of being a center of handmade shoes in Korea, Seongdong-gu launched the Handmade Shoe Industry Revitalization Project for Seongsu-dong for a long time. The efforts of the district culminated in the Joint Handmade Shoe Market and a newly designed, shoe-themed subway station, both of which opened to the public on December 13, 2013.

Get off the Seoul Metro at Seongsu Station on Line 2, and you will discover elevators decorated with drawings and patterns of shoes. The station has been transformed into Shoespot Seongsu, which displays and promotes the industry of handmade shoes and their products in Seongsu-dong. Exit the building, and you will discover a sculpture of a cat, in a red dress and high heels, sitting atop a gigantic pair of golden boots. Right behind this artwork, named "The Red Dream of a Cat," is "From SS", the central venue where you can purchase quality handmade shoes from local artisans. From SS, featuring seven box shops on the ground floor of the Seongsu Subway Station, is a joint market of handmade shoes featuring products from shoemakers officially recognized and certified by Seongdong-gu. In a tiny space at the end of this store, named "Shop 7", you will find a man making shoes, as intent as he has ever been over the last 55 years.

Right behind this artwork, named "The Red Dream of a Cat," is "From SS", the central venue where you can purchase quality handmade shoes from local artisans. From SS, featuring seven box shops on the ground floor of the Seongsu Subway Station, is a joint market of handmade shoes featuring products from shoemakers officially recognized and certified by Seongdong-gu.

# The Tanned Hands of Seoul's
## First Master Shoemaker

—

With its aspirations to become the "Bologna of Seoul"—as the Italian city is famous for the quality leather goods and shoes it produces—over and beyond the domestic capital of shoemaking, Seongdong-gu decided to find and designate local shoemakers with excellent skills as master shoemakers. Having enacted the Municipal Ordinance on the Designation of, and Support for, the Master Shoemakers of Seongdong-gu, the district organized a public contest in November 2013, inviting skilled artisans to compete so the district could find a master shoemaker proud of his art and capable of making a contribution to the advancement of the local shoemaking tradition. Yu Hong-shik emerged as the winner of this contest and became Seoul's first officially recognized "Master Shoemaker."

The shop may be small, but it is not without class, particularly with its elegant and luxurious handmade shoes on full display. On one wall, you will see a bronze plaque bearing the inscription, "Seoul's First Master Shoemaker," along with a photograph of the shop owner holding the award he won in the 2013 contest. Visitors come in every now and then, surveying the shoes on display. Yu gets off his seat to explain his shoes in detail to such visitors when necessary, but his hands remain fixed on the shoes he was making throughout the entire interview. As if his hands were meant for shoemaking only, Yu never lets go of the leather and other shoemaking supplies. The light beige leather in his hands takes on the shape of a shoe in no time. The leather is a tough material that unskilled hands cannot easily pierce through even with the strongest needle they can find. Yet, in Yu's hands, the leather appears as soft and pliable as satin, with his needle moving in and out in a comforting rhythm. This kind of ease can come only from decades of mastery over one's art, and it is impossible not to admire it.

**You must be in your 60s now. How have you been able to be in this line of work for 55 years?**

I began making shoes when I was about 12 years old. I was born and spent my childhood in Gwangju, Jeollanam-do, but moved to Seoul very early on.

**What made you move to Seoul so early in your life?**

It's not like I have a dramatic story to tell, about how poor my family was and such things. I am almost ashamed to confess this, but I never liked school and learning when I was little [*he chuckles*]…After deciding that I had no future in school, I agreed with my friend to go to Seoul and learn a trade for living. The trade I chose was shoemaking.

**Where did you first start working?**

It was a company called Gineung Jehwa, located in Myeong-dong, the center of Seoul. The company was famous as one of the best producers of handmade shoes in Korea at the time. I learned this craft with dedication and passion. I worked so hard that I began to garner respect and even teach others at age 19.

**You must have been a prodigy at shoemaking if you were able to teach others so early. It must have taken more than effort.**

As I think about it, my folks were good at doing things with their hands. I see this ease with handicraft in my father and grandfathers as well as in my kids. We must have been born with something. We are good at making things with our hands and also have a quick eye so that we can glance at something and learn it immediately. Of course, we are also hardworking people.

**That kind of talent must have prompted you to start out on your own.**

After learning all that there was to learn, I returned to my hometown in

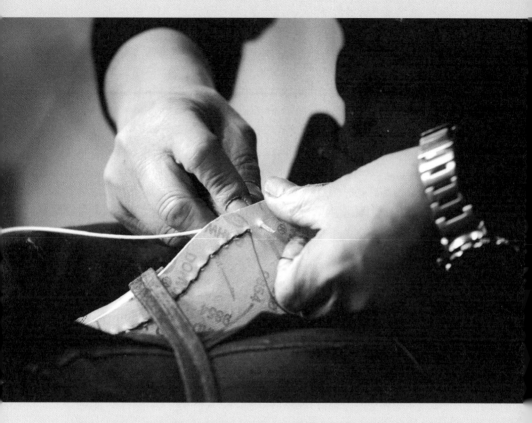

The leather is a tough material that unskilled hands cannot easily pierce through even with the strongest needle they can find. Yet, in Yu's hands, the leather appears as soft and pliable as satin, with his needle moving in and out in a comforting rhythm.

Gwangju and set up my own shoemaking shop. I had countless customers who treasured the shoes I made for them. I became well-off in just a matter of years and kept expanding my business for decades after that.

**You were a huge success in Gwangju, so why did you come back to Seoul?**

That kind of success was not enough to rescue my business from the aftereffects of the Asian Financial Crisis. I had been expanding it rather aggressively before the crisis, and lost everything I had when the crisis finally broke out. I barely managed to bring my wallet with me when I decided to relocate to Seoul again. It did not take me long to re-establish myself in Seoul again, though. After decades of hard work, I now own a small home of my own. I paid for the education of my children and also encouraged my wife to do what she has always wanted to do. Things have worked out well for me.

**You did experience hardship, but you trusted enough in your skills to re-start.**

That is absolutely right. I owe all that I have now to the skills I have learned. You have no idea how grateful I am and how much pride I take in the fact that I am able to earn my living with the honest work of my two hands. There are many people who lie constantly and deceive others for their own gain. Every time I meet such people or hear about them on the news, I look down at my hands. Look how honest they look! I know I earn all my living honestly and conscientiously. That is the biggest source of my pride.

Yu then stopped what he was doing and reached out his hands for me to see. He could not have looked more confident. The kind of look on his face was something I could see only on the faces of people who were deeply satisfied with their ability and skills. With such strong hands and face, he survived and prospered in this rough world, proudly raising his family on honest work.

# "I am not just a manual laborer."

___

His shop is designed so that passersby can easily find him at work behind the glass windows. To catch a glimpse of this honest old man concentrating steadfastly on the work at hand impresses and inspires people. Yu is a paragon of a working man. Seongdong-gu must have gotten the same impression from watching him at work, as it was the district that created this special workspace for Yu and asked him specifically to work here so as to raise the reputation and profile of Seongdong as a shoe town.

Yu received a plaque recognizing him as the first official master shoemaker of Seoul from Mayor Park Won-sun at the opening ceremony for From SS and Shoe Spot in December 2013. Predicting that Yu's name will be remembered as an icon of handmade shoes in Korea, the mayor asked Yu to continue with his dream of becoming Korea's "Testoni."

**It must have been quite an honor to receive that kind of recognition.**

I kept thanking the mayor and the head of Seongdong-gu for giving me such an honor. I wasn't just being polite. I was truly grateful. I never imagined that I would become someone officially recognized and honored by government authorities. I felt as if all the hardships I had suffered had been compensated. Few in Korea ever took an interest in what I do or my trade.

**It is true that Korean society tends to look down upon technicians and manual work.**

I agree. That is just how the world works. One day, I had a meeting with an insurance salesman. In trying to estimate my daily income, he wrote me down as a "manual laborer." I could not believe my eyes and felt quite angry. But I tried to stay calm and told him quietly to forget about the entire business.

"There are many people who lie constantly and deceive others for their own gain. Every time I meet such people or hear about them on the news, I look down at my hands."

I cannot count the number of times I felt humiliated and compelled to feel shame about my work. In those moments, instead of taking out my anger on people, I just returned to work silently and focused on making shoes until I regained calm.

**Yes, so think of what a great change it is for the Mayor of Seoul and city officials come to you, asking you whatever they could do to help you.**

You are right. I just wish that this had happened to me and other shoemakers much sooner, though. Had society given us the recognition and respect we deserved, and had the government supported the shoemaking trade as part of Korea's manufacturing sector, we would have developed better shoemaking techniques and produced even more quality products.

**What is it like to work in shoemaking and the distribution of handmade shoes?**

Things are not as reasonable or fair as we would like. Most of my clients take the goods I make and pay me much later. Old customs and practices like this make it quite difficult for producers like me to survive long on the market. And the amount of orders we get is in no way regular or predictable. I have had countless colleagues who complain to me how difficult it is to raise their families and plan their future on the amount and kind of income they earn. I do not think skilled shoemakers in Korea have ever enjoyed the gains they truly deserve for their mastery.

**Are you saying shoemakers in Korea are overskilled for what they earn?**

That is exactly what I am saying. Korean shoemakers are top-notch worldwide. Koreans used to beat competitors from other nations all too easily in past international skills competitions. After Korean shoemakers claimed all the gold medals, shoemakers from other countries decided to forfeit and never return to the competition. The easy victory Korean shoemakers had was what

*Yu said he could not stop thinking about new designs and inspirations for shoes. While walking down the street, eating lunch, in business meetings, and even trying to fall asleep, he kept thinking of new shoe designs.*

led the competition organizing committee to abolish the shoemaking category altogether.

Yu's hands kept moving busily with the leather and thread throughout the interview. At one point, however, he suddenly stopped and raised his voice.

"Italy may be famous for its luxury handmade shoes, but I do not think products made in Korea are of any lesser quality. We can easily beat the Italians in terms of quality and skills and make Korean handmade shoes the most highly respected in the world."

He began to survey the shoe rack next to him and picked up a pair. It was a pair of red leather ankle-high boots, with thin stretches and leopard-patterned, furry belts of cow leather around the top.

"Look at these boots and see their design and quality. I designed them myself. These are unique boots you will never find anywhere else. I have made countless models and designs of shoes that others never thought about. I am certain that I can compete with any master shoemaker from around the world."

As a matter of fact, the designs of the majority of shoes on display in his shop are entirely his own. More than a dozen pairs of shoes kept tempting me with their unique and sophisticated look. Yu said he could not stop thinking about new designs and inspirations for shoes. While walking down the street, eating lunch, in business meetings, and even trying to fall asleep, he kept thinking of new shoe designs. He confessed to having a bad memory and that he could not even remember the telephone number of any of his family members. "Yet," he said, "I cannot forget the designs of shoes I barely glanced at while passing a shop window. The memories of these shoes are incredibly vivid."

# Keeping Alive the Embers of the Shoemaking Tradition

——

Yu easily beat seven other skilled candidates at the shoemaking contest and became Seoul's first officially-recognized master shoemaker. He had no qualms about the series of assessments making up the contest, for he had confidence in his skills. Assessing the sole he made for a shoe, the referees of the contest could not help but admire: "Here are the embers of Korea's shoemaking tradition!"

They were particularly impressed with Yu's *tteuk-gaboshik* technique. This technique of shredding the whole animal skin into pieces to create leather shoes has its origin in the way Koreans made their straw sandals generations ago. Yu says this was a technique that shoemakers commonly used back when he first started learning his trade. There are few living shoemakers with the knowledge of this technique today. Shoemaking is a dying trade and few are willing to learn and inherit this and other handmade shoe techniques.

**As a master craftsman, you must feel sad about the current situation.**

I have always feared that there would be no one left to practice this trade after I retire. Korean shoemakers possess unique and great skills, and I would be really sad to see all these skills and traditions completely disappear because no one is willing to learn them anymore.

**Are you interested in taking apprentices and teaching your trade?**

That is the last wish I have to fulfill before I retire. I have been waiting for talented and committed young people to appear and learn this craft from me. The apprenticeship model of the past may no longer work in today's reality, but learning this craft will still take enormous amounts of time and dedication. Thankfully, I have a student who has been learning from me for three years

*As a matter of fact, the designs of the majority of shoes on display in his shop are entirely his own. More than a dozen pairs of shoes kept tempting me with their unique and sophisticated look.*

already now. I also have a student who owns a shoemaking shop in Japan and visits me regularly to learn this and that. In order for future generations to learn handicrafts, however, we need support on the public and systemic level as well. If Mayor Park, Won Soon does succeed in opening up a shoe academy as he has promised me, I will be happy to volunteer my time there.

**You have been working for the last 55 years. Don't you want to take a break?**

Why not? I would like to retire any day now and return to my hometown to reunite with my childhood friends and also travel around the world with my wife. Now that I have been named a master shoemaker of Seoul, though, I sense a greater burden on my shoulders. It is not easy to distill what I know about my trade and pass it down to the next generation. I guess I should not think about retirement any time soon.

**You are a talented and respected shoemaker. Haven't you ever thought about taking your business abroad?**

In the past, I dreamed of going abroad to countries like Italy to learn more about the shoemaking art and compete with experts worldwide. One day, though, a feature article on handmade shoes I read in a magazine woke me up to reality. The shoemaking tools and process described in that article were not much different from the ones I used at the time. That is when I realized this simple truth: I could make the world's best-quality shoes wherever I was.

A shy smile came over Yu's face. One who has accomplished something and earned one's own self-respect need not seek validation through comparisons with, and praises from, others. Yu knew that true talent would be recognized anywhere in the world.

"I have always feared that there would be no one left to practice this trade after I retire. Korean shoemakers possess unique and great skills, and I would be really sad to see all these skills and traditions completely disappear because no one is willing to learn them anymore."

# A Love Affair for 55 Years

—

Random visits by potential customers punctuated the interview every now and then. Yu's shop specializes in men's shoes, so it is no wonder that the majority of guests visiting his shop were men. At one point, two very sophisticated-looking young men stepped in. They stayed quite long, carefully studying the shoes on display. They asked Yu the prices. A subtle look of dismay appeared on their faces after Yu told them. Shaking their heads, the young men stepped out.

A pair of shoes made by Yu can fetch a price ranging from hundreds of thousands of won to millions of won. Yu's shoes are not for everyone, but the prices seem fair for the designs, quality, and the amount of effort Yu puts into making them. After all, these are shoes designed and created by Seoul's Master Shoemaker.

"I have no intention of lowering the prices of my shoes. Just think of the kind of material and the amount of effort that go into the making! Customers are used to paying fortunes for the imported shoes on display at high-end department stores. Why should they think any differently about the shoes that master artisans like myself make?"

Then an elderly gentleman appeared. He seemed more interested in Yu's art and skills than in the shoes on the racks. The man appeared to know the true meaning and value of handmade shoes. After watching Yu at work intently for a while, the old gentleman asked Yu: "How many pairs of shoes do you *build* a day?"

Without ceasing his *building* process, Yu answered, in a polite voice: "I build about two or three pairs a day."

Yu starts working at five o'clock every morning. He owns a shoemaking

*One who has accomplished something and earned
one's own self-respect need not seek validation through
comparisons with, and praises from, others. Yu knew that
true talent would be recognized anywhere in the world.*

factory in Seongsu-dong, not far from his shop. After working for several hours at his factory first, Yu moves to his box shop around 10 a.m. and stays there until the evening.

**You look quite healthy for your age and work schedule. You look much younger than you are! Are you sure you are in your 60s now?**

Thank you, I'll take that as a compliment! It must be because I do what I enjoy most.

**Have you ever gotten tired of your work?**

I have never regretted choosing this trade as my lifetime career. I love shoemaking more than anything else in the world. I would never trade this for anything, even for a Harvard degree!

Yu then picked up the hammer made of birch wood—glossy from wear—that was sitting next to him and began to pound the sole he was making. A satisfied smile appeared on his face. He is a true master shoemaker who takes pride in his calloused hands and honest work.

You will be surprised to discover this man who continues to make shoes completely by hand after 55 years in the center of Seoul. He has been a master craftsman long before anyone recognized and honored him as such.

*I would not trade*
*this honest work of shoemaking*
*for a Harvard degree.*

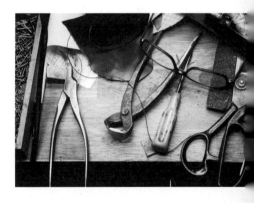

Kim
Jong-eun

—

Master Bag Maker
42 years of work

# Happy Craftspeople Make Masterpieces

—

| | |
|---|---|
| 1959 | Born in Yeongdong, Chungcheongbuk-do, Korea. |
| 1974 | Began working, at age 16, at a handbag exporting company in Seoul. |
| 1991 | Became a master sewing machine operator, but quit due to poor working conditions and began working onboard a deep-sea fishing vessel instead |
| 1992 | Returned to sewing and began making handbags in Japan for 17 years. |
| 2006 | Returned to Korea and began creating handbag design samples. |
| 2008 | Opened up a handbag craft workshop in Jungnang-gu, Seoul. |
| 2014 | Founded Songgong, a luxury handbag brand for women (www.songgong.kr). |
| Present | Continues to run Songgong and advises handbag designers and manufacturers. |

Kim was waiting for me when I got off the bus near his workshop. The neighborhood I arrived at was in Ogeum-dong, and it had taken me repeated transfers between subway rides and local buses to get there. Kim Jong-eun, my interviewee for the day, is a master bag maker with 42 years of work behind him. Like Kim Do-yeong and Yu Hong-shik, the master craftspeople I interviewed earlier, Kim has also dedicated many years to perfecting a single craft. The sheer length of the period of time they have spent on their respective crafts alone probably qualifies them for the title "master". Kim, however, has a unique history. At one point in his career as a skilled bag maker, he quit and had a brief stint working on a deep-sea fishing vessel. Of course, he returned to his craft, but this time settled in Japan, where he ended up making handbags for 17 years. Wanderlust appears to have ingrained his veins. I was excited for this interview with him, as he seemed full of dramatic life stories to tell.

## "I am who I am today because of the efforts I have been making to improve my surroundings."

——

Kim was scouted by the company he is working at today about two years ago, when he was running his own workshop in Jungnang-gu, Seoul. He has expert knowledge of the entire process by which a handbag is born, from design and patternmaking to sewing and production. Today, he is working as a patternmaking expert, focusing on the design phase of handbag production. He sits on the board of his company as an executive director, but he prefers to be thought of as a "teacher" instead of a director. In any case, he is an undisputed master bag maker.

**You are in your mid-50s now. How have you been able to work in this field for 42 years?**

I began working at the head office of a handbag exporting company in Seoul when I turned 16 years old. I was not a particularly bright student at school, and would get scolded by my father every once in a while for spending my time on making things with scrap wood rather than on studying. Anyway, I was confident in my ability to create things with my hands from an early age, and started working in this line of work, probably too bravely, thinking I didn't need to study hard to get far ahead.

**Even today many avoid working at factories because the work is hard. It must have been worse back in your days.**

All I can recall whenever I look back on those times is how much hardship and struggle I had. I began working in this field from the very bottom up, not even knowing whether I was paid my fair due for the work I did. I was simply grateful for the fact that the company that hired me fed me and gave me a room to stay, while also teaching me a craft I could use later in my life. I was paid once every two months back then, but did not know I was poor. I just kept learning the craft, thinking a better day would come eventually. I learned by copying the works of more skilled workers, and by reviewing the patterns I had learned during the day in my own room at night.

**You were so young and must have felt tempted to quit. How did you last so long?**

Even today, I believe that learning is something one can do even outside schools. So when my friends and coworkers drank their paychecks away and gambled on horseraces and other such games, I stayed in my room and tried to learn patternmaking and English.

**You seem to have strong self-discipline. You did not allow yourself to**

**become lazy or complacent. You must have learned your craft quite quickly.**

I shouldn't boast too much, but, yes, I am the type of person who always strives to reach the next level after accomplishing something. At first, I began my career as a mere assistant, doing everything that my superiors told me to do. Even then, though, I worked with the clear goal of learning the sewing machine techniques. I eventually became what people call the *oya-missing* ("master sewing machine operator"), but then I ran into a wall. The more I worked, the more I came to compare my station with those of others, and wondered what I should do differently to get farther ahead in my life. We all worked hard, but some managed to accomplish much more while others stayed in the same positions. I kept wondering why.

**What about now?**

Now I feel that there is no higher position or level I should strive to reach. This craft I have learned and practiced for decades is the biggest asset I have. I am who I am today because of the efforts I have been making to improve my condition. I am proud of the work I have been doing. This craft has not earned me any great fortune, but I do not regret a thing.

**You may be a born hard worker, but haven't you ever experienced old customs or the structure of this industry holding you back from achieving greater success?**

Of course I have. I set up and ran six subcontractor factories, but they all floundered in the end, due to the difficulty of finding workers and the meagerness of the profits. While running those factories, we would also meet bad customers who defaulted on payments they owed us. I was weak and had no course of appeal. Things have changed much since those days. Society appears to be changing for the better, albeit very slowly.

Kim wanted me to indicate that he, along with hundreds of thousands

"The more I worked, the more I came to compare my station with those of others, and wondered what I should do differently to get farther ahead in my life. We all worked hard, but some managed to accomplish much more while others stayed in the same positions. I kept wondering why."

of people working in manufacturing and handicrafts, worked hard for the industrialization and economic development of Korea during the 1970s. Koreans today think that the sudden economic boom at the time came about as a result of a few select industries only, such as textiles and electronics, but Kim remembers that handbag manufacturing was an equally indispensable and booming industry at the time. He wants his hard work to be remembered by today's generation of Koreans.

## Risking Life to Survive the Dark Hours

—

The more I talked with Kim, the more I came to conclude that he was a natural hard worker, never the type who would swerve to other lines of work or career opportunities just because he was fed up or things were not going his way. So I could not help wondering how he came to leave this craft and decide to work in something entirely different. Kim told me that the handbag exporting company he worked at also owned a wig factory. It was not uncommon to see such factories of handbags and wigs in downtown Seoul back when Kim was young. The young Kim strove day in and day out to learn as much as possible about his craft, with the hope that a better day would eventually dawn on his life. He wasn't asking much with this humble hope, but the reality appeared to be resistant to change. After years of working in his field, he realized that he was not earning enough to raise his family. Poverty and fatigue never went away, no matter how hard he worked.

**Is that why you decided to work onboard a deep-sea fishing vessel?**

I had to find some other, and hopefully better, way of raising my family. I was so disappointed with my situation that I just wanted to leave Korea. So, when I turned 30 years old, I quit my job and got work onboard a deep-sea fishing vessel that caught squid. My job was to pluck endless rows of squid from the fishing wires from an automatic roll located on the hull of the ship. I slept three hours a night and ate six meals a day on that ship. My days there were the darkest hours of my life, and I risked my life to survive those dark hours.

**Things were not much better on water, were they?**

That's right. At one point, it dawned on me that, if I were to work so hard and suffer just the same, I should work and suffer on land instead of on water. The time I spent onboard the fishing vessel was full of pain and fatigue, but it taught me a valuable lesson. Having survived such a time of despair onboard a ship, what more could I not endure? I am grateful for this lesson I took away from that job. Every time things did not go my way, I recalled this lesson and kept persevering.

**And you finally returned to bag making, didn't you?**

That's correct, but I did not want to work in the same environment I had left. That is why I moved to Japan in 1992, not knowing a single letter of *katakana* or *hiragana*. While working in Japan, I learned the language and finally came to set up my own factory on the outskirts of Tokyo.

**You stayed in Japan for 17 years. Something must have been working right for you.**

Things were much better there. I must have had some luck and found a large corporation willing to hire me as their contractor. The Japanese have far more respect for bag makers than Koreans do. I was satisfied with what I was earning. But I returned to Korea in the end, in 2006. This time, I started working in making design samples for bags.

**Has the working environment here changed much since you left?**

*Kim wanted me to indicate that he, along with thousands of hundreds of people working in manufacturing and handicrafts, worked hard for the industrialization and economic development of Korea during the 1970s. Koreans today think that the sudden economic boom at the time came about as a result of a few select industries only, such as textiles and electronics, but Kim remembers that handbag manufacturing was an equally indispensable and booming industry at the time.*

*"There is no next generation of bag makers to inherit what we have accomplished so far. Five to ten years from now, Koreans will be forced to import bag makers and technology from abroad."*

Not very much. Koreans still insist on getting things done as soon as possible. That insistence on speed is what undermines quality and the chances to learn and improve techniques. Consumers are ultimately the ones who pay the price for this compromise. They pay high prices for their bags, but do not get the quality they deserve.

**How can we expect the current level of bag making technology to remain intact in Korea, let alone hope for the technology to improve in such an environment?**

Almost no one in Korea today wants to learn the bag making craft. There is no next generation of bag makers to inherit what we have accomplished so far. Five to ten years from now, Koreans will be forced to import bag makers and technology from abroad, directing our orders to factories in other countries. Handbag making today is not as hard as it used to be in the past. There are more people working in this field today with better education than their predecessors ever had. But today's college-educated bag makers do not have the patience to withstand and stay in the current working environment. This field offers little hope of a better life in the future, and the starting salary is meager, ranging somewhere between KRW 1.2 million and KRW 1.5 million a month. Newcomers are forced to work long hours, often amid the toxic smell of glue and other harsh working conditions. My generation persevered in a much worse environment and for much lower pay, but that was because we had no other means of putting food on our tables. The pool of future workers for this industry is shrinking day by day. I wish I could say something more optimistic about the future of this field, but there are simply too few people today who are willing to put up with all these absurdities.

**Isn't there any public system supporting the education and development of the next generation of bag makers in Korea?**

I have heard that the Korean government has begun to provide grants and loans for small shop owners and craftspeople, but most of us have almost no knowledge of how to work computers and also have little education. The administrative procedure for applying for such grants and loans is often too complex and cumbersome for us. Given the workload we have to handle, we can barely find time to read newspapers and learn what goes on in the outside world.

This sentiment was something held in common by all the craftspeople I met for the interviews for this book. The bad working environment with no sign of radical improvement, low pay, unfair structure of distribution, and an administrative support system that alienates the intended beneficiaries all serve to contract the pool of young people willing to learn the crafts. With few young people entering the fields, craftspeople struggle to find ways to keep their crafts and knowledge alive and growing. When the current generation of craftspeople is gone, a core part of the manufacturing infrastructure in Korea will collapse, thus accelerating the erosion of the industries and markets in this country.

## With the Death of the Cottage Industry Comes the Death of a Nation
—

Kim thinks of himself as a top-class master craftsman. He takes great pride in his career and skills, and is duly recognized by others as well. He created handbags and totes for the First Ladies in the past, and recently produced a new briefcase for the current President. There is almost no one who would question or doubt Kim's reputation as Korea's master bag maker.

**In your opinion, what are the qualifications that a master bag maker must have?**

To become a master bag maker, one must be able not only to do everything involved in the process, but also to do everything well. The entire process includes pattern designing and making, leather cutting, polishing and refining the leather using machines, applying glue, and a host of other activities. A true master is someone who is capable of doing each and every one of these activities with perfection. I would say there are fewer than two dozen such bag makers in Korea capable of doing all this. I could probably count on one hand those who are capable of carrying out the entire process on their own with perfection.

**I see few women in bag making. The work must be physically exerting.**

If I were to compare the two processes, dressmaking probably requires one-third the work required by bag making. Much of bag making involves the use of leather, which requires great amounts of physical exertion that women may find out of their physical ability to handle. We used to have many women working in this field back in the 1970s and the 1980s when Korea was a major exporter of handmade bags. Few remain in this field today, though.

**What is it like to work in the bag making industry today?**

Most factories are small-scale workshops hiring three to five people each. I rarely see factories with more than 10 employees. The demand for our products continues to decline. Distributors keep placing small orders out of a fear of accumulating inventories. The majority of people in this field work for minimum prices and pay. More and more bag distributors and manufacturers in Korea have their products produced in developing countries with cheap labor. We have already begun to import more bags than we export now. There are few signs of hope for the remaining craftspeople in Korea today.

*The bad working environment with no sign of radical improvement, low pay, unfair structure of distribution, and an administrative support system that alienates target beneficiaries all serve to contract the pool of young people willing to learn the crafts.*

**But aren't the working conditions in the field better? I hear that employees at many companies today work only five days a week.**

That may be the case with established businesses, but apply little to subcontractors. Subcontractors cannot afford to take all weekends off like others do. The less they work, the less they get paid. How can they afford to take weekends off, then? They are forced to work every day to earn a minimum living.

**I guess working for well-established shoe brands is a subcontractor's best option?**

The majority of subcontractors already working with such brands hardly enjoy better conditions. A friend of mine, who runs a bag making factory, recently complained to me that, after collecting all the payments he was owed and paying up his employees, all he had left in his hands was KRW 170,000. I have travelled far and wide around the world, and can say this for sure: with the death of the cottage industry comes the death of a nation.

There is another, structural, factor that undermines bag making factories in Korea. Kim blames large corporations here, which have no qualms about making headway into the specialties of cottage industries so long as doing so makes money. Small shops and factories thereby increasingly lose the ground on which they can stand.

These large corporations invade the existing order and ecosystem of cottage industries without any serious understanding or long-term vision, and leave the industries with equal ease when they stop making money. In the meantime, small shops and factories are left almost destitute, forced out of the lines of work in which they have striven for decades.

# All Masterpieces Contain the Breath of Their Makers

—

We headed for Kim's factory, about a two-minute walk from his office. Handbag manufacturers in Korea are concentrated in the central part of the country, especially Seoul and the small cities of Hanam and Bucheon in Gyeonggi-do. The number of factories in Seoul easily outnumbers factories elsewhere: there are over 200 factories in the neighboring districts of Junggok-dong, Myeonmok-dong, Junghwa-dong, and Manguri in Jungnang-gu alone. The majority of these factories, however, are located underground, earning the region the nickname, "the Underground Industrial Complex."

Kim's factory was one of these underground shops facing the main road. The owner of his company, a man named Gu He-hoe, was working there with two other employees. Gu was working with his sewing machine when we got there, sewing a piece of quality leather onto a wooden plank to make a suitcase. The young male employee and the female employee—I later learned that she was a Chinese immigrant of Korean descent—were applying glue onto the leather.

The factory was filled with the horrid smell of glue. It was a spacious place, allowing for much air, but the smell in it instantly reminded me of the odor of glue that hung about the shoemaking factories of Yu Hong-shik and Yang Yeong-su, also interviewed for this book. If the smell of glue is what bothers bag makers, the thick layer of dust in the air is what bothers dressmakers and seamstresses. Ventilation is a crucial matter in manufacturing.

Gu welcomed me, but without leaving his sewing machine. All the while he and I talked, he kept working the leather, his glance only occasionally leaving the sewing machine to meet my eyes. He related to me a telephone conversation he had the day before. "This young guy called me up out of the blue yesterday.

Gu was working with his sewing machine when we got there, sewing a piece of quality leather onto a wooden plank to make a suitcase. The young male employee and the female employee were applying glue onto the leather.

He said he was a recent college graduate, having majored in fashion design. He wanted to know if I would let him come here and learn the bag making craft. I kept telling him not to come. Why should he bother learning the craft of a dying industry?"

**(To Gu) You told the young man that because you knew there is little hope for this industry. But wouldn't you say things would get better if more and more young people learned and entered this craft?**

I have no intention of teaching my own children this craft, so it would be dishonest if I told others' precious kids to learn this craft. Of course, we would be happy to see young people willingly learn and inherit this industry from us, but I do not want to make them work in the same working conditions I face now. The end is already written in the book. This industry is dying, and I do not want to lead young people to think and hope otherwise. Of course, I cannot deter truly determined people from entering this field and making new attempts.

Kim, who was standing nearby, picked up the bag Gu was sewing and told me: "Look at this part. With two or more runs of sewing, this bag would be much better in quality. But we don't—no, we cannot—do such additional sewing because our distributors don't want that. With additional sewing, the price would go up. Distributors don't see the need for that, since people are willing to buy much lower-quality bags anyway."

Kim then challenged me to guess how much of the final price of the bag would go to the bag maker. As I continued calculating and estimating in my head, Kim finally said: "It's six percent! A meager six percent of the price of this bag falls to us. I would be the happiest man on earth if I could receive 10 percent of the price."

**Why don't bag makers in Korea unionize? They would be able to raise their voices then.**

I am a straight shooter and cannot hide what I think from others. I can say pretty much anything I want to say because people still want my skills and advice. Few people in this line of work, however, ever want to or can afford to dare speak the truth. If others built a bridge, they would be willing to walk that bridge and cross the river to the other side, but they seldom want to build the bridge together.

**Given your experiences abroad, you probably compare the working conditions in Korea to those overseas.**

Yes, I do, even though I don't want to. I had chances to visit the factories of luxury bag brands in Italy and France. There several skilled craftspeople share a spacious workspace, each calmly working on or sewing his material. Time does not matter for them, as their clients are willing to wait for a whole month or even longer until a bag is finished. These craftspeople have the luxury of taking coffee breaks every now and then and enjoying the scenery outside their window. They truly enjoy working, watching the seasons pass and nature work its wonders outside their window while they work and sew the leather.

**By contrast, bag makers in Korea are forced to work in windowless rooms under the ground, smelling glue all day long.**

Yes, and so many eventually give up and leave this field. They possess this amazing craft and skills, and are willing to work hard, but cannot support their families on their income. Nine out of ten bag makers live in rented homes. I know numerous skilled bag makers who are separated from their families and live alone in small, dismal rooms. This is the hard reality facing the people who have dedicated their lives to learning and perfecting their craft and made Korea's exporting industries prosper in the 1980s. Why do we have to suffer so much for having lived such hardworking lives?

The gloomy look on Kim's face and the sorrow in his voice kept haunting me on my way back home from the interview. All masterpieces contain the breath of their makers. Given the same amount of experience and skills, which artisan would be able to make a better product: one who has enough time and leisure at his disposal and therefore has been able to focus his soul onto the product he has been making, or the other who is forced to stay in an under-lit room, breathing in air heavy with the smell of glue to finish making his product as soon as possible? The difference in working environment translates into the difference in quality of the resulting product.

Luxury goods often hide the pain and sorrows of artisans who are rarely paid what they truly deserve for their skills and labor. How much time an artisan can spend on making a product bears close correlation to the quality of the product he makes. A masterpiece is not just born overnight under a pair of skilled hands. The label, "handmade," describes goods hand-crafted with care and dedication by artisans who are treated and respected properly, and not the goods mass-produced by the "mechanized hands" of underpaid and time-pressed workers.

The interview with Kim taught me that happy craftspeople can make masterpieces. As consumers, do we not have a duty to care about the wellbeing of the makers of our bags?

*Luxury goods often hide the pain and sorrows of underpaid artisans who are rarely paid what they truly deserve for their skills and labor. How much time an artisan can spend on making a product bears close correlation to the quality of the product he makes.*

# It Takes Both Craftspeople's Own Efforts and Government Support to Create a Brighter Future for Korea's Dressmaking Industry

### Park Gyeong-mo (Chairman, Seoul Apparel and Dressmaking Cooperative)

The areas around 657 and 42 in Changshin-dong, Seoul, are respectively Korea's largest sources of women's and men's clothing items that are sold both at home and abroad. In the middle of Changshin-dong, a new place has been erected for Seoul's dressmakers. It is a place where people can stop by for a coffee break and gather together to find effective solutions to problems that affect them all. The building houses the Seoul Apparel and Dressmaking Cooperative (SADC), which local dressmakers and factory owners created together in 2012.

I am serving as the Cooperative's chairman now. The SADC's organization includes the Chair and the Vice-Chair, the Head Operating Committee and its Chair, the Senior Director, the Advisory Board, and the Auditor's Group. The organization is divided into the Planning, Business, Training, Public Relations, Women's, and Design Divisions. Each division has an operating committee, on which six to nine executives sit. There are about 60 people working for the Cooperative today, including executives, the Secretary-General, and managers on the administration team.

### From a Friendly Gathering of Nine People to a Cooperative of 240 Members

Our office may look small and humble to others, but we at the SADC are proud and excited to have our own working space finally. The Cooperative was launched only a few years ago, but many members of the Cooperative have known and been working with one another for a long period of time. Ours is the first cooperative for dressmakers in Seoul, so we get many visitors and inquiries that seem to reflect our growing stature and importance in local affairs.

The formation of a cooperative was a surprise for many dressmakers as well, who spent their youth industrializing Korea in its heyday during the 1970s. There was an association of dressmakers before the SADC, but the association lacked effectiveness as it was too loose and focused solely on satisfying individual interests.

Yet it was almost by happenstance that the SADC came into being. The founding members, including myself, did not have any specific plan to organize such a cooperative from the beginning. In 2008, Seoul provided free computer training classes for dressmakers. Most craftspeople working in this line of work are computer-illiterate and feel that they are out of date. The computer classes were therefore a great opportunity for us to learn a new skill and also to become acquainted with one another. Twice a week, from 9 to 11 at night, we took the computer class at 647 Changshin-dong. That is why we named our gathering "647" at first, which initially included the nine owners of local dressmaking factories who took the computer class together for three months. After the class, we would get together at nearby pubs, enjoying barbecued meat and a few drinks, and occasionally joined by local passersby as well.

Almost two years went by, and our gathering had grown to almost 200 members or so. With such a large number of people, there was growing demand that we organize ourselves and apply our gatherings and activities to productive ends. In August 2012, we finally came to form the Apparel and Dressmaking Solidarity Society. The organization remains intact to this day, with the members regularly meeting in the second week of each month. In other words, we started as a gathering of nine friends, came to organize our own association, and finally arrived at today's cooperative form.

Prior to launching the Cooperative, we briefly entertained the idea of founding an incorporated business, with about a dozen members, each putting down an initial investment of KRW 3,000,000. As we looked around for possible investors, we were able to recruit 21. I was excited to discover that there were more of us than I thought who were willing to take and share the risk of starting up a new venture. After some discussion, the investors-to-be finally decided to organize a cooperative instead of a corporation.

We began our preparations for launching the Cooperative halfway through 2012, and held our inauguration assembly in December that year. We received the government's authorization the following January. To become a member, one must make an initial investment of KRW 100,000 in the Cooperative. We currently have 240 members, and the number is steadily rising. There are almost 500 members who attend the monthly gatherings of the popular Apparel and Dressmaking Solidarity Society, paying the monthly membership fee of KRW 10,000 each. Not all of these 500 people have become members of the Cooperative because the required initial investment can be quite a burden to some people.

**Sharing Work via Joint Shops and Factories**

On the ground floor of the SADC building is a small apparel shop, which was made possible, along with the SADC office, through a grant from the Small and Medium Business Administration for craftspeople. The shop displays and sells clothes made by 15 of the Cooperative's members. The SADC factory will also open by the end of 2013. With the joint factory, we will be able to share orders, work more effectively, and enjoy greater income security as a result.

We owners of small dressmaking factories all deal with the whims of the market directly. We make clothes as ordered for fixed fees. We have difficulty determining the fees ourselves, as clients can always go to other dressmakers who offer lower prices. There is therefore growing anticipation and hope among dressmakers about the upcoming joint dressmaking factory of the SADC. Once such a factory is established, we will be able to receive large-scale orders for uniforms and other such items of clothing from institutions and corporations and share the workload among ourselves. At present, the dressmaking factories we operate are mostly small-scale, employing only three to five people each, and forced to stay idle in between orders. There are numerous such factories and dressmakers who spend much of their time waiting for new orders in Seoul today. Therefore, it would indeed be great if we could organize ourselves and join our resources and capacities together to secure large orders, the workload from which we could divide among ourselves. Being organized is advantageous not only in terms of securing new orders, but also in influencing fees. Unionization offers a number of advantages that are not available to individual craftspeople.

Yet this business of running a cooperative has turned out to be much costlier, in terms of both money and time, than we imagined. We had an initial capital of KRW 63 million, which was not enough for us to secure an office space and a shop. We began to amass additional investments from members, and finally raised an additional KRW 125 million. Along with the initial capital, we now had almost KRW 200 million in our hands, and could not let that amount of money sit idly by in a bank account. We then set out to find new profit-making opportunities.

We began to brainstorm. At first, we thought about supplying the essential goods that our dressmakers typically needed each day. One example is the instant coffee available in small packets. Each packet of instant coffee is sold for KRW 120 or so at typical supermarkets. If we could place a large order for the coffee packets and pay in cash, we could lower the price to KRW 100 per packet. Then we could redistribute the coffee packets to our members for KRW 110 per packet, and generate revenue for the Cooperative in return. This system of bulk sales soon extended to thread, yarn, ribbon, adhesive tape, volume-rate garbage disposal bags and other such materials and items that our members need and use daily.

We also seized on the fact that most of the members in our organization were originally from rural towns. They still had their parents and other relatives growing various crops in their hometowns. So we decided to trade the farm produce from these rural towns directly to the members, charging only minimal intermediary fees. This direct trade system benefitted both farmers and the Cooperative's members. We try to do thorough market research before selecting and selling any such farm produce because the Cooperative as a whole makes only a meager amount of income from such sales, most of which should be reinvested in the Cooperative's daily administration.

## Growing Need for Low-Rent Apartment-Type Factories and Better Working Conditions

The most important concern of the SADC is the welfare of its individual members. There are over 1,600 dressmaking factories in the district of Jongno-gu alone, including those working under the table, according to a survey from July 2013. Changshin-dong by far houses the greatest number of these factories. There are 980 factories in this area, each capable of conducting the entire dressmaking process from cutting to sewing. The entire area of Changshin-dong depends upon dressmaking for its livelihood. Yet we dressmakers face increasing struggles and challenges in today's recession-prone economy. I see fewer and fewer motorcycles running along the alleyways of Changshin-dong these days. There are about 2,500 motorcycles registered in my neighborhood. When the dressmaking industry was booming, so many of these motorcycles were out on the street, carrying fabric and other such goods, that pedestrians could hardly walk without having a close call or having to stop. These days, however, with the dressmaking industry in decline, the streets and alleyways of Changshin-dong remain free of motorcycles.

As the chairman of the SADC, I feel increasing pressure on me to find more work for the Cooperative's members to do. We dressmakers have different specialties. Some are good at making blouses; others, at blazers; and still others, at pants. Each factory only tends to specialize in the production of one category of clothing. The dressmaking factories in this neighborhood are so good at their respective specialties that they can process an order in a single day, releasing the finished products by evening. If a client places an order for hundreds of dress shirts of a specific design, a single factory can make all those shirts, catering perfectly to the client's taste and specifications, in a single day. I hear that this kind of practice or system is unique to Korea. This is possible because we dressmakers have access to everything we need here in Changshin-dong, including the fabric shops, shops for dressmaking tools, and even factories that specialize in the finishing touches.

The only problem is that all these factories specializing in different items are scattered across the neighborhood, thus limiting the extent to which all the related dressmaking processes can be integrated. What if we had an apartment-type dressmaking factory here in Changshin-dong? Dressmakers on one floor could specialize in making pants; others on another floor, in making shirts, etc. Such a factory will dramatically streamline our working process and enable us to process even more orders than we do now. With people working in the same trade thus gathered and united, we will also be able to improve our working conditions.

Improving our working environment is a top-priority concern for us now. After making clothes, we have unbelievably large amounts of scrap fabric. All this leftover fabric is garbage, and we struggle daily to dispose of it. We put all of it into volume-rate garbage disposal bags, and the bags come out so bulky and heavy that we can hardly carry them to the spots on the street designated for garbage disposal. Elevators would be of great help to us, as they could help us save all those trips up and down the staircases. But we dressmakers mostly work in tiny and worn-down buildings that lack elevators. Given the nature of our work, our factories are also always filled with dust floating in the air. Few are willing to work in such a dusty environment until late at night.

Politicians have been sloganeering and campaigning, ostensibly to make our working environment better. I have doubts, though, that their effort has substantially improved our working conditions. The Dongdaemun Biz Center was created, but the rent is too high for us even to dream of moving in there. Every election season, candidates running in the mayoral race or for local councils promise that they will create a new facility where we can all enjoy a more pleasant working environment, but we know that the chances of such promises being kept are slim at best. Land prices in Seoul continue to soar, while the dressmaking industry is in continued decline. We wish Seoul would create a public apartment-type factory for us to rent, but this wish may never come true.

### The Dressmaking Industry in Crisis: Solidarity Is Crucial for Breakthroughs

The dressmaking industry in Korea is struggling so much that I fear there might not be a dressmaking industry to speak of in 10 years. Few are willing to learn and inherit our trade. Back in our days, we were eager to learn this trade for poor pay, bearing so much humiliation and even physical beatings. We have dedicated major portions of our lives to mastering and perfecting our craft. Among the members of our Cooperative, one who has worked in this industry for 28 years is the youngest.

Of course, the Korea Academy of Fashion and Sewing, founded with the initiative of Assemblywoman Chun Soon-ok, and the Small and Medium Business Administration offer various trade-related programs, classes and lessons. Few of the students enrolled in these programs, however, envision spending the rest of their lives working at dressmaking factories. The majority of trainees at these institutions take these classes not to specialize in dressmaking, but to set up their own clothing repair shops. In the past, a high school diploma would have been considered an educational attainment in this industry. Today, the majority of people newly entering this field have college and university degrees. The younger generation today simply has less patience to bear with the working conditions that the older generation gladly suffered.

We founded the SADC because we dressmakers felt an acute sense of alarm at the seeming decline of the dressmaking industry in Korea. The Cooperative factory and the joint shop represent only part of our endeavor for finding breakthroughs out of the current rut.

The SADC exists ultimately to improve the welfare of its members. Its primary concern, however, is to increase the amount and stability of income for its members. We are also considering plans for collaboration with other industries, such as handmade shoes. As far as the big picture is concerned, our hope is to find ways to ensure a better livelihood for all craftspeople working in the manufacturing sector in Korea. I must confess, though, that I do not yet have a clear blueprint as of now that shows us how we might get there.

One of my favorite occasions is the celebration we hold at the end of each year. All the dressmakers we know are gathered at a single venue to meet with and encourage one another. In the contours and wrinkles of these dressmakers' faces I see the shadows of the past year characterized by challenges and hardships. On such an occasion I recall how busy we have been throughout the year, so busy that we could hardly find the time to meet up with one another and share our personal sorrows and complaints. The SADC exists so that we can share our burdens and challenges in a more organized and systematic manner to continue building a brighter future of the dressmaking industry in Korea.

**About Park Gyeong-mo**

It was in 1979, when he was 19 years old, that Park first entered the dressmaking world of Changshin-dong. Park started out helping his uncle, who was running a small clothing factory back then, not knowing that he would find a lifelong career in his first job. Having lived and worked in Changshin-dong for 36 years, Park decided to do something for his fellow dressmakers and the younger generation of dressmakers, and thus accepted the request to head the newly born Seoul Apparel and Dressmaking Cooperative. Park is also the owner of a small factory specializing in the manufacturing of women's pants. He goes to his factory early every morning, and then handles multiple meetings at the Cooperative office in the afternoon. Now also serving as Vice-Chair of the Council for the Welfare of Urban Fashion Craftspeople, organized in October 2014, Park is busy looking for and devising measures to promote effective collaboration among local dressmakers. Working in so many jobs, Park feels tired and overburdened at times, but sees increasing signs of hope in the growing movement these days toward reviving the vitality of the Dongdaemun area and the dressmaking industry in Korea.

There Will Be No Future for the Korean Fashion Industry
without Craftspeople Being Properly Treated First
Jang Hyo-ung (Master Patternmaker, 43 years of work)

I Could Make Shoes Even with Fallen Leaves
If People Were to Recognize the True Value of My Work
Yang Yeong-su (Master Shoemaker, 37 years of work)

Current Status of Traditional Jewelry Craft in Korea:
Excellent Jewelry Makers, Poor Distribution Support
Kim Sang-sil (Master Jewelry Craftsman, 25 years of work)

# CHAPTER 2

# Can we just get a word?

# Jang
# Hyo-ung

—

Master Patternmaker
43 years of work

# There Will Be No Future for
# the Korean Fashion Industry without
# Craftspeople Being Properly Treated First

—

| | |
|---|---|
| 1955 | Born in Seoul. |
| 1973 | Began working at the Andre Kim boutique. |
| 1979-2007 | Worked as production manager, patternmaker, etc. at Korea's best high fashion boutiques, including Lee Gwang-hee Boutique, Miss Park Tailor, Kim Jeong-a Boutique, Luciano Choi, and Lee Won Jae. |
| 2007 | Became head patternmaker at No Brand and began teaching at the Korea Academy of Fashion and Sewing. |
| 2009 | Became Vice-Chief of the Office of Development at Hansol Textiles. |
| 2014-Present | Continues to teach the next generation of expert clothes makers as senior director at the Korea Academy of Fashion and Sewing. |

The Korea Academy of Fashion and Sewing is located in a worn seven-story building, standing right in front of the Dongdaemun Subway Station. The Academy offers programs for the next generation of clothes makers in this building and also at its main office located on the fourth floor of the nearby Seoul Design Support Center. It was at the Academy that I decided to meet and interview the master patternmaker, Jang Hyo-ung, with 43 years of work behind him and still teaching future patternmakers. Jang's voice soon filled the entire conference room, next to the sewing practice room filled with dozens of sewing machines. I could detect a combination of both resignation and resolution in the criticisms and condemnations he spewed out. What has filled the heart of this seasoned patternmaker with such rage and sadness? Captivated by the force of his stories, I could not help but continue listening to him.

## No Retirement for Craftspeople
—

Having just entered his 60s, Jang is one of the most skilled and respected patternmakers alive in Korea today. The dresses he designs and makes are praised far and wide for being "seamlessly perfect." He retired from his main job recently, not because he wanted to, but because the company he was working for asked him to retire. Speaking of this experience, he could not hide the severe look of disappointment spreading over his face. That disappointment was indeed earned, because this man still felt that the value of the skills and expertise he possessed transcended the age barrier.

**You are by far the most respected patternmaker in the country. So you must be really upset that you have been forced to retire.**

Thanks to the activities of powerful auto unions, much controversy and public rage has erupted over plans Korea's auto companies seem to be entertaining of relocating their production facilities overseas. The apparel industry in Korea has an even greater added value than the auto industry, but we see no such fuss over apparel workers being laid off because we have no unions in this field. Companies can dismiss skilled workers almost at will, and the dismissed employees have no recourse except to pack up their belongings and leave their workplace of decades right at that moment. There should be no "retirement" for craftspeople as long as they keep their wits intact and can offer valuable services to industries and society. But the company suddenly asked me to leave — to retire, to be exact. I know I can easily find work out there, just like other skilled craftspeople. But I cannot get over the brazenness and rudeness with which the company decided to let me go.

**Your anger seems to be directed at the treatment accorded craftspeople in general in Korea.**

There is little ground on which skilled dressmakers can stand in Korea today. Apparel companies here have all relocated their production overseas in search of cheaper labor. In the past, only large corporations could do that. Now even small businesses access overseas manufacturers and craftspeople with almost equal ease. They even have their samples made overseas. I once saw a TV program that introduced a prosperous apparel company. The TV host gave high praise to the judgment of the company's management to relocate overseas and cut costs. What company can we call "Korean" if it handles all its manufacturing and production abroad?

**Are you saying that these companies' decisions to move overseas amount to abandoning Korean workers and the Korean manufacturing sector altogether?**

"*Labor may not be as cheap as it once used to be in Korea today, but stopping production here will ultimately force all skilled workers and craftspeople out of the market. What is going to happen in the future as Korean apparel companies now have even their samples made abroad?*"

Labor may not be as cheap as it once was in Korea today, but stopping production here will ultimately force all skilled workers and craftspeople out of the market. What is going to happen in the future as Korean apparel companies now have even their samples made abroad? Once Vietnamese and Indonesian workers learn enough of our techniques, how many buyers will there be worldwide who would be willing to come to Korea and place orders?

**Isn't sample making about creating a perfectly finished product before placing it in mass production? Doesn't it involve the use of much knowledge, skill and technique?**

You're right. Sample making is indeed the final and most important step of the pre-manufacturing dressmaking process. It requires the input of the most skilled artisans. So I have a hard time understanding how Korean apparel companies could have so easily relocated sample making overseas just to save pennies. Isn't it foolish? I may not have much education, but know enough to call that decision foolish. How can company executives not know what I know? Why don't they put their education and brains together to find a better way? Policymakers should enact a law requiring companies to maintain part of their production in Korea if there is any increase in their sales. Under such a law, companies will be forced to maintain production in Korea and continue hiring Korean workers, and skilled craftspeople will not need to worry about their livelihood and future as much.


A born straight shooter, Jang had no qualms about speaking his mind. He cannot help but speak the truth. He has experienced much frustration and despairs in his life, and may have learned the value of speaking his mind whatever the cost may be. But that is not the only reason. He is able to raise his voice because he believes he is qualified to do so.

# "You have only a middle-school education!"

Luckily enough for him, Jang began his career at a young age at the best fashion boutiques in Korea at the time. Having worked and learned for two years at an Andre Kim boutique, Jang soon moved to Miss Park Tailor, where he worked for another nine years. There are few well-established designer shops in Korea Jang has not worked at. Jang was then scouted by a large apparel company and worked for years as Korea's highest-paid and most talented patternmaker. Powerful and famous people in Korea, including statesmen and numerous first ladies, have worn clothes perfected by him.

A few years ago, Jang began to teach classes at the Korea Academy of Fashion and Sewing upon my suggestion. I wanted to revive the Dongdaemun apparel industry, and believed that talented and qualified teachers at the Academy could facilitate that revival. Students at the Academy have been the biggest beneficiaries of this initiative so far. Jang was eager to help out because he also agreed with me on the importance of keeping the clothes making craft and techniques alive in Korea. But administrators failed him once again, demanding from him written records of qualifications, such as licenses and school transcripts.

**Formalities and procedures are the backbone of bureaucracy. Even knowing that, you must have felt frustrated often.**

As you know, I have been teaching at the Academy for the past eight years. Then I heard from others that city officials and bureaucrats of other government departments go around asking about us, raising questions about whether we are truly qualified to teach. Why do we need licenses? If anything, we should be the authorities capable of granting licenses! The City of Seoul, the Ministry of

Industries, the Ministry of Employment and other such government agencies know nothing about how things work in this field. That is why they keep demanding useless "proof".

**Why doesn't the government take the initiative of according the right treatment and respect to craftspeople? That way, the entire society can better learn to change their perception of craftspeople.**

You cannot simply compare seamstresses, patternmakers and other such craftspeople to college graduates and doctors. We learn and use our knowledge in different ways. No matter how skillful we are and how valuable our skills, we will never earn as much as people with doctorates do. That is how society works. It keeps telling people like me: "You have only a middle-school education! How dare you earn more than people with doctorates?" Skills and techniques are treated here as not deserving of as much respect as book learning.

**What do you think of the salary we pay you at the Academy for teaching?**

When I first began teaching the hand-pattern class, I was paid KRW 100,000 per hour. Then a city official filed a complaint, saying my fee was too high. My pay was halved beginning the subsequent semester.

**It was an offense to a master craftsman like yourself. Why did you not quit?**

How could I? After all, I have to impart knowledge and skills!

Until he retired recently, Jang went to work by day and taught classes at the Academy by night for eight years. He invested so much of his time, effort and passion into teaching, but saw little improvement in the treatment he was receiving at the Academy. Nevertheless, he had small comfort in the fact that he is spending more and more of his time on advertising the Academy and raising public awareness of the importance of the clothes making craft in Korea.

*Having just entered his 60s, Jang is one of the most skilled and respected patternmakers alive in Korea today. The dresses he designs and makes are praised far and wide for being 'seamlessly perfect'.*

# Why "Andre Kim" Can Never Become "Chanel"

—

A living witness to the history of Korea's fashion and textile industries, Jang began to explain the ups and downs of that history in a plain manner. According to him, the first Western-style modern fashion boutique in Korea emerged about six decades ago.

"The history of modern Western-style clothing in Korea began with Roh Ra-no. Look at what has happened since then. Mr. Roh is alive today, but who remembers his clothes or his shop? What about Chanel, that French fashion brand beloved all over the world? Coco Chanel died decades ago, but the brand 'Chanel' still thrives today. We have legendary fashion designers still alive in Korea, but few today remember their designs or clothes. Why?"

**Yes, that is indeed curious. Coco Chanel died, but her style is still an inspiration to countless women worldwide. Why doesn't the same happen with Korean fashion brands?**

That is because Korea does not educate and train expert designers, patternmakers, tailors and dressmakers. Chanel treated her craftspeople well, so much so that they remained loyal to her vision even after her death and helped her brand survive and succeed. Chanel keeps hiring talented designers from around the world and different generations, but the basic framework—the Chanel spirit—lives on unchanged. The same seamstress cuts fabrics and the same patternmaker makes patterns down the generations, keeping the Chanel spirit alive for decades. These craftspeople also impart their knowledge and expertise with pride. After Andre Kim, that most renowned of Korean fashion designers, passed away, what has happened to his clothes? His vision and style have completely disappeared into oblivion. That is the reality of fashion design in Korea today.

**Are you saying it is craftspeople that kill or keep alive the value of fashion brands?**

Yes, I am, because fashion is all about the skills of the hands. A designer brand may manage to survive for a generation or two, but it will soon vanish if its craftspeople leave and the clothes produced under its brand name are no longer of the same quality. I want to tell fashion designers: Treat your craftspeople right if you want to keep the quality of your clothes the same.

**Fashion used to be treated as a concern and luxury of only a few in the past in Korea. The Korean government, however, has begun to enact various measures to foster fashion, textile and related industries today. What are your thoughts on the government support for clothes makers?**

There is no such thing as government support for clothes makers. All that policymakers care about is to find new genius fashion designers. Of course, the more shops new designers open, the more work we craftspeople would have. But people often forget that novice fashion designers do not have the means to hire expert pattern or dressmakers for good pay. As these designers struggle with rents and a host of other expense items, they end up hiring less-skilled clothes makers for less pay, settling for sewing and patterns of lesser quality. How can fine-quality clothes come about in such an environment? The government should turn its attention to clothes makers as well, providing grants and other forms of direct support.

**Senior craftspeople, like yourself, must have a role to play in that regard.**

I do acknowledge that, and have begun to make new attempts at the Academy and elsewhere. I have begun to make patterns for much smaller fees for up-and-coming designers. I want to work with young people. I want to tell them with my work: "Think of this world as your stage. Let me help you make better clothes!"

**Young designers must be very surprised to learn that they could have you —after all, one of the most well-paid clothes makers in the country — make patterns for them. There are many readers out there who still do not know what patternmaking exactly is in fashion. Could you explain to us what your job is about?**

If we could compare a finished piece of clothing—a blouse, a jacket, a dress, whatever it may be—to a tree, patternmaking is akin to its root. We patternmakers produce good patterns and show them back to designers, telling them silently with our work how clothes should be made. I wish I could help startup brands find their unique styles and lines. I can help them be and remain creative with the patterns I make. That's what I intend to do from now on.

**This book will be published, and people will read what you have just said as a public promise. Are you alright with that?**

How can I not keep my promise, when I have already told everyone I know about my new ambition? These days, I keep telling myself not to be so hung up on how well I was paid in the past, and to start doing meaningful, satisfactory work for myself and others. I keep asking my friends to remember to punch me in the face if I ever show them signs of obsessing over money.

**Don't we need a bigger and better system in order for talented craftspeople like yourself to impart their knowledge and skills throughout the related industries?**

Before we begin to build a new system, we first need more people like me. To encourage people to become like me, we need to pay them better. The government may do more to secure adequate income for craftspeople, but corporations can also help by raising funds for encouraging and training skilled craftspeople. If businesses themselves are unwilling to help, we craftspeople

"*These days, I keep telling myself not to be so hung up on how well I was paid in the past, and to start doing meaningful, satisfactory work for myself and others. I keep asking my friends to remember to punch me in the face if I ever show them signs of obsessing over money.*"

need to unite together and mobilize our resources so as to keep our tradition and skills alive down the generations."

**I guess that's where the Academy comes in — you know, in order to teach and produce the next generation of skilled craftspeople.**

You must know because you hired them, but all the teachers at the Academy are the most respected leaders of their respective fields today. We often hear students saying that this place is different from other schools they have experienced. My wish today is for the Academy to become a central agency of practical training and learning programs for colleges and universities. Actual craftspeople need to stand at the podium and teach students majoring in fashion and related subjects. That way, we will begin to see more and more talented and skilled designers.

While teaching at the Academy, Jang has written numerous textbooks on patternmaking and dressmaking. He is also a co-author, along with university professors, of such books as *Skirt and Pants Patternmaking* (Ahn Hyeon-suk, Bae Ju-hyeong, and Jang, Hyo-ung) *Jacket Patternmaking* (Ahn Hyeon-suk, Bae Ju-hyeong, and Jang Hyo-ung) and *Patternmaking* (Bae Ju-hyeong and Jang Hyo-ung), all from the publishing house Iljinsa. The pride Jang takes in his skills and trade is evident in these books.

# "In order to survive, fashion designers must learn to partner up with craftspeople."

—

Jang counts himself as exceptionally lucky among lifelong patternmakers. He also credits his perseverance for his success. He is proud of the fact that he has supported his parents and raised good children, and also owns a home now, all on the income he has earned making patterns. His wife has been his biggest supporter throughout his adult life, so he says he has nothing to be envious about.

**Anyone interested in patternmaking has probably heard of your name. You must have had struggles and hardship before you got to where you are today.**

In Korea, crafts and trades have always been the destiny for children of poor families. These children grow up and acquire all these great skills and trade-related knowledge, but they can barely escape poverty even as grownups. I also came from such a poor family, renting a single room for a large family with several kids. At one point, I worked four part-time jobs a day. I even set my room on a fire by falling asleep while reading and studying under candlelight.

**What does it take to become a patternmaker?**

You can't just glance at an experienced patternmaker at his job and learn instantly. You have to start by doing the miscellaneous assistant work in the field, often for years. You can begin making your own patterns only after you master the entire process of clothes making. I began by learning to cut and tack fabrics at a fashion boutique. It takes people between five and 10 years doing such work before they become patternmakers on their own right. Many leave the field halfway through such process, about three years after starting to work.

**But aren't patternmakers the most well-paid of all clothes makers?**

To an extent, that is true. Once you become a skilled patternmaker, you have greater chances not to worry about your financial future, but how much you are paid will also depend on how skilled you are. Of all people working in clothes making in Korea today, about a tenth are patternmakers. You may become and gain recognition as a patternmaker, but it will still take you years or even decades until you begin to earn good income on that fact alone.

**I heard that you have also taught your son to become a patternmaker.**

When my son was little, I never pressured him to study hard, but only kept telling him to be and remain healthy. I am thankful that he has grown up to be such a healthy man. After he completed his military duty, I took him under my tutelage and began to teach him the basics of patternmaking. After about a year or so, I noticed that he was also learning by himself. But it took him 12 years in total to become a skilled and recognized patternmaker. Today's colleges promise to produce patternmakers in just two years. Why are they lying?

**You know better than anyone that this path is filled with difficulties and disappointment. So I am curious what made you decide to bequeath your craft to your son.**

Yes, it may be extremely difficult to become a well-recognized patternmaker, but I still believe that this profession has prospects. More importantly, though, I wanted to share the joy of making patterns with my son. Science and technology may have made much progress, but there are still many things that require human hands. Computers are also increasingly used in patternmaking today, but it is ultimately human hands that perfect and finish patterns. With the flood of newer and better machines today, patternmakers in the field are required to learn and study harder than ever. Even so, I believe in the value of human hands.

*Jang is a master patternmaker who has been making the basic
roots of clothing all his life. He has been working with silky,
smooth fabric akin to the wings of angels, but he strikes other
people as a man of strong character, with moral fiber and
skills to support such a strong stance.*

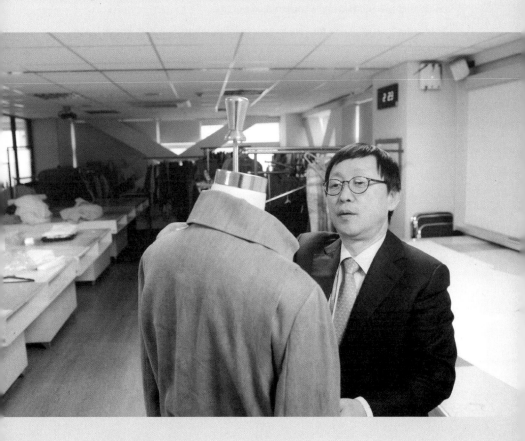

**Like father, like son. You two must have a lot to talk about as professional partners as well.**

My son is now working at a company that imports and exports clothes. He is a grownup man now, but has no qualms about phoning me up right away to ask any questions he has. These days, I can explain things mostly in words and he understands, without me ever needing to show him how things work. He has had ups and downs in his career, but I am very proud of the fact that he has taken after me and become a patternmaker.

**This is the final question for you: In your opinion, what counts as a good piece of clothing?**

A good piece of clothing is one that captures and reveals the beauty of the natural curves and lines of the human body. Cheap clothes do not fit the body well because underpaid and unskilled clothes makers do a careless job with sewing and patternmaking. SPA fashion brands are in vogue these days, but consumers know that clothes from such brands never last long. They are poorly made and of unspeakable quality. People eventually gravitate toward well-sewn and well-fitting clothes.

**How do you project the future of the Korean fashion industry?**

There will be no bright future for the Korean fashion industry without according craftspeople their due treatment and respect. It is about time that globally renowned fashion and designer brands emerged in Korea. After all, what other products can we sell to consumers worldwide? We have to convince consumers worldwide who want to buy and wear Korean-made clothes. How can we foster such brands and designers to emerge? We need to foster craftspeople first. The profile and stature of Korean fashion brands remain second-tier on the global stage today, and I believe that is because the Korean fashion industry has failed to treat its craftspeople right. More and more Korean apparel companies focus on copying fashionable designs instead of making genuine investment in crafts and skills. How can we become world-class when we fail to accord the respect due to our own craftspeople?

Jang is a master patternmaker who has been making the basic roots of clothing all his life. He has been working with silky, smooth fabric akin to the wings of angels, but he strikes other people as a man of strong character, with moral fiber and skills to support such a strong stance. He has spent more than 40 years making patterns and clothes, but patternmaking still strikes him with joy and wonder every morning. How can we let people like him retire? At age 60, he still has eyes that sparkle with as much excitement and curiosity as those of a little boy. Even after retirement, he continues to build the roots of the Korean fashion industry.

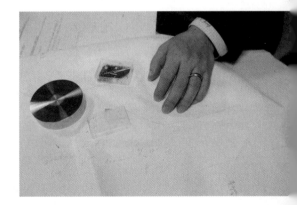

Yang
Yeong-su

—

Master Shoemaker
37 years of work

# I Could Make Shoes Even with
# Fallen Leaves If People Were to Recognize
# the True Value of My Work

—

1965      Born in Pyeongtaek, Gyeonggi-do.
1979      Entered the world of men's shoes by working as a clerk at a salon shoe store at
          Geumho-dong, Seoul, at age 14.
1988      Began to make women's shoes after becoming a shoe patternmaker at a salon
          shoe store at Seongsu-dong, Seoul.
2006      Founded Scoall Shoe Company.
2011      Joined the Joint Handmade Shoe Store at Seongsu-dong, Seoul.
2012      Began teaching shoemaking at the Small and Medium Business Support Center
          at Seongdong-gu, Seoul.
Present   Continues to run Scoall Shoes and teach classes.

"You have to cover up this whole part and raise this other part to make the shoe you want. Men's shoes should look heavy and serious in order to be stylish."

Yang Yeong-su, an expert shoemaker, continued instructing one of his students in the shoemaking class he was teaching at the Small and Medium Business Support Center (SMBSC) at Seongdong-gu, Seoul, when I visited him. The district of Seongdong-gu began to provide shoemaking training and classes for interested participants in 2012 in order to maintain and revive the local shoemaking industry. About a dozen or so local expert shoemakers, with 30 to 40 years of work behind them, have volunteered for this program. Each of these volunteers teaches a class for six months on end, teaching their disciples the entire process of shoemaking, from sharpening the knives and working the machines to the handling of the exterior leather and the soles. Yang comes to the center to teach a class three times a week. He spends the entire afternoon at the center every day when he comes in.

The classes on offer are intense. Trainees are required to attend classes in theory and practical training from 10 a.m. to 5 p.m. every day except for Sundays for six months. Any trainee who misses three of the required classes is automatically expelled from the program. On the wall of a classroom I visited were strict signs that read "No Earphones Allowed" and "No Social Media Allowed." Even without these signs, however, the trainees, mostly young people in their 20s and 30s, would have focused solely on the shoemaking techniques they were practicing. The strong smell of glue did not seem to bother them at all. Each trainee was working on creating a pair of men's shoes and a pair of women's shoes that they were required to present at the graduate works exhibition in the last week of their program. The trainees' eyes sparkled with the determination to emulate their master teacher's far superior techniques.

# If I Could Focus on Making Shoes Only

—

The Handmade Shoe Town in Seongsu-dong, Seoul, is a unique place that gathers the designers, makers, sellers and marketers of locally produced handmade shoes that consumers can directly access and purchase. The town currently houses 350 or so shoemaking companies, all of which together hire more than 3,000 people. The Seoul Seongdong Shoemaking Association opened up a joint handmade shoe store in June 2011 for local shoemakers. It provides a business space for 25 companies today. The Association has even gone on to recruit franchisees and dealerships nationwide, hoping to encourage the creation of similar venues and handmade shoe towns across Korea. What does our master shoemaker, with 37 years of work behind him, think of this effort?

"Well, I think the shoe town should have something more unique. It should be known to people as the place where they can find unique and original designs unseen anywhere else. We need to make this place a venue for introducing rare and innovative shoe designs. I am not sure it is there yet, though," he says.

**The local government and district office have begun to provide support. What do you think of that? Is the handmade shoe industry showing any signs of recovery?**

I see few signs of hope for the manufacturing industry for now. Clients try to keep prices as low as possible. Suppliers refuse to grant manufacturers lines of credit. We manufacturers are caught in the middle, trying to make both ends meet. We are often strapped for cash and eventually come to lose our credit with our clients. In the past, I made salon shoes, which earned me quite an amount of money—at least more than other kinds of shoes. These days, I make almost no profit of my own on any shoes I make. Back then, I was at least able to do whatever I wanted to do with shoemaking. The manufacturing sector in Korea, however, has been in decline for many years now, with no signs of improvement. We shoemakers try to innovate and create new things, but often at the risk of not receiving the fair prices we want. That is why few shoemakers are willing to create anything of high added value these days.

**You have your own shoe brand, "Scoall," but also continue to receive orders from other shoe producers for manufacturing, correct?**

Yes, such orders from other shoe companies for generic designs with mass market appeal still form the majority of the work we do at our company. But this arrangement is still rife with unfair practices and absurdities. A client, for example, who places such an order calls the lowest possible price, saying that we could do it with that price if we bought our supplies from a particular dealer somewhere in Dongdaemun. However, that Dongdaemun dealer is willing to give us the low price we need only if we were to visit the dealership in person and pay everything in cash. Yet small manufacturers like us can hardly find the time or the money to do so, while our client will not pay us until two months after we finish his order.

**How about the Joint Handmade Shoe Store at Seongsu-dong? Consumers would be happy to come there, as they could find shoes of great quality and original design at much lower prices than at department stores.**

We producers put the same shoes up for sale, only with different labels, for half the normal price, but consumers would still not buy them. Consumers prefer to pay twice as much for well-known shoe brands even though they are the same quality as ours. I understand that, but still wish things were different. We handmade shoemakers set up this store because we were greatly struggling alone and decided to gather our resources together. For an endeavor like ours to succeed, though, we need a lot of customers. We have yet to work on that.

**You mean the government needs to make the support it provides for manufacturers more substantial and practical from the perspective of actual management. Have you ever benefitted from any government or public support?**

Yes, I have, about seven years ago when I set up my own company. I took a government loan for new entrepreneurs, and another loan afterward for management support. I have paid back both loans almost in entirety. These loans charged me much less interest than bank loans, so they were of great help to me. I do not want free help. I just wish the government would give me some room to breathe, by lending me enough for rental deposits, for example. I have heard somewhere that such a program exists, but I fear the paperwork involved. And I would have to have a good credit score even to apply for such loans, but I don't, so that is another problem.

**Yes, paperwork can be prohibitively cumbersome.**

I know that I could probably receive government grants and loans if I submit good paperwork. But people like me have worked for so long only in doing things with our hands. Even the word "paperwork" gives me a headache. Rather than spending our time figuring out how to access and borrow the money we need, we choose instead to focus on making new shoe samples. Even though I am often strapped for cash, I do not go around asking for money owed to me, but think only about making new hit samples. That is what craftspeople are. We are good at doing things with our hands. We do not have a particular aptitude at borrowing and making money.

The stylish, European-inspired joint shoe shop at the Seongsu-dong Shoe

District now generates upwards of KRW 100 million in monthly revenue. This means that a tenant business earns about KRW 10 million or so a month. Much of that revenue, however, goes toward paying for expenses and production costs. That is why the tenant businesses, even after three years, continue to struggle to make ends meet. Yang tried to sound optimistic, saying that we should find hope in the small improvements being made.

## Don't Think You Can Support a Family Solely with This Trade

—

About 70 people applied to join the shoemaking program at the SMBSC. The center chose 12 of them, none with any prior experience with shoemaking, for intensive training. Taking the classes on offer for four and a half months may be enough for trainees to become familiar with the terms and required skills, but they will still need much more practical training, through years of hard work in the field. Even after years of practicing their skills that way, they will still be seen as "rookies" to expert shoemakers like Yang, who know that mastering a trade can take decades.

"Master craftspeople are not created overnight. Mastering a craft requires a constant willingness to learn. Even after finishing one's formal education and training, one should strive to know and learn more to master one's trade. What improvements and progress can come from a person who is content with what he knows today and never strives to learn more?"

**What other criteria do you think shoemakers should satisfy?**

A shoemaker must love shoes and be willing to invest all the time he has in

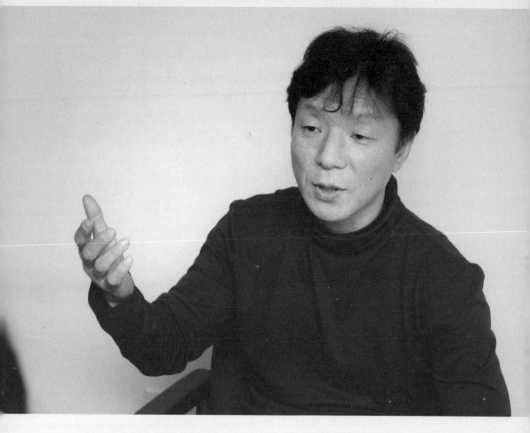

"We producers put the same shoes, but only bearing different labels, at half the prices, but consumers would still not buy them. Consumers prefer to pay twice as much for the same-quality shoes bearing well-known brand labels. I understand that, but still wish things were different."

making the shoes he dreams about. The only thing I want to tell people who might be interested in this trade is this: Don't think about raising your families on this trade alone. Manufacturing is in such dire straits in Korea today that you cannot adequately support a family even if you master shoemaking.

**How were things for manufacturing in the past?**

When I first entered this field, shoemaking was a craft that not everyone could learn and master. Back then, people highly valued handmade salon shoes, and we craftspeople were accorded high pay and much respect. We were able to demand prepayment and also charge high prices on our products. Manufacturing was booming at the time. These days, few want to work in manufacturing, and the remaining craftspeople are hardly given the respect and treatment they deserve. True master craftspeople deserve respect and recognition. I have never dreamed of making much money, but I wish I didn't need to worry about day-to-day living, having mastered and specialized in this trade for so long. The reason Koreans no longer produce quality handmade shoes today is simple: it is because they are not paid for working hard and making good shoes. That is why they do such slapdash jobs, content to work as mere apprentices.

**That hardly satisfies anyone, whether producer or consumer.**

Pardon me—I think I may have been a little harsh in what I have just said. Let me give you an example to make this easy. Think of those fussy ceramic makers. They create a pot and smash it on the ground if they do not like it. Just as there are ceramic pots that their maker cannot decide whether to keep or to throw away, there are shoes that their maker cannot decide whether to present to the consumer or to throw away. My personal belief is I should throw away, without any hesitation, the shoes that I dislike even a bit. Yet under the current system, I cannot act as I want due to the price and cost factors. Consumers themselves do not have a discerning eye to recognize what kinds of shoes are well-made. Unless they have made the shoes themselves, they would not detect flaws with these shoes. I myself had no discerning eye almost a decade into practicing this trade.

**Are you saying that the quality of handmade shoes in Korea is going backward?**

I still vividly remember this incident that I saw at the beginning of my career. One day, I came into the shoe shop where I was working, and saw the shop owner cut away at the pair of shoes that my teacher had made, saying such flawed shoes should not even be seen on the market. The shoes looked perfect to me or to any other discerning eye, and would have been sold without any problem on the market today. These days, few shoemakers are willing to put as much effort and care into making their products as my teacher was at the time. Who would be willing to do so much work for so little pay? To get quality shoes, we should pay the master shoemakers much more than what we pay them now and give them enough time to perfect their products.

# Shoemaking Is Still the Most Exciting Thing to Me

—

Yang began making shoes at age 14 alongside an older second cousin who was working as a shoe patternmaker at the time. Yang fell in love with this trade at first sight. He says he has never felt tired of this craft. He is a born shoemaker.

"Shoemaking is still the most exciting thing to me now. I have no weekends or holidays. Other shoemakers may take a break from time to time, but I come to work almost every day. I come here even when I have no work to do."

**You must love learning at your job.**

I was excited every day when I first started learning this craft. Back then, crafts like shoemaking were not for everyone to learn and adopt. There are endless streams of people looking to enter this field, but senior craftspeople would not take up disciples unless they were bright and showed some potential. Only the bright and the hardworking could learn crafts like this.

**Entering the field of a handicraft must have been as much a subject of envy as it is to enter a large and well-established corporation today. But I am sure it took you much more hard work than talent to get as far as you have gotten.**

Of course it did. How could I progress without striving to learn and develop my own ideas and skills? I finished learning everything I needed to learn from others in just half the time that it took others to learn. I prepared everything even before my teacher told me to do anything. I had a great teacher who was really strict and never allowed his trainees near the sewing machine before they got to a certain level of knowledge and skills. So I would practice my learning on the sewing machine in secret, stitching thread into scrap pieces of leather. I worked hard day in and day out to master this craft, and still remember the joy I felt when I became a teacher of my own right. Of course, the higher pay I got for being able to teach and train others was a boon, but I was most delighted because I felt that others recognized my skill and talent.

**I had heard that a strict apprentice system used to exist in the shoemaking industry.**

Yes, it did. Back then, hard work and good skills were not enough: you had to have "pedigree." Fellow shoemakers cared about at which salon shoemaking factories you worked and for how long. If you worked under a strict and well-known teacher for years, you needed not submit any other qualifications to find a job in this industry. Shoemaking companies also cared about personality and character of their job applicants.

**So you have satisfied all those criteria and finally landed a position at one of the most famous shoemaking companies at Myeongdong, haven't you?**

England, Kim's, Debon were some of the most revered, legendary producers of handmade shoes at the time. If you spotted a particularly stylish man or woman walking down the street at Myeongdong, he or she undoubtedly had on a pair of really nice shoes. Even two decades ago, I made a pair of shoes with genuine ostrich leather which cost KRW 1.3 million.

**That was possible because people knew the true value of handmade shoes back then. You must have enjoyed your work greatly at the time.**

Yes, I did! I made all these gorgeous and perfect shoes then. Even now, I feel excited to touch real quality leather. It makes me love my work all the more. I try to take my time with costly leather, repeatedly wiping away any minute traces of glue I might have left on it. I cannot allow even the tiniest defect mar the product I make with such fine material.

**Things are different for shoemaking today, aren't they?**

The popularity and stature of the shoemaking industry peaked in the 1970s, but began to decline in the 1980s and afterward. But I remember the manufacturing sector booming until the mid-1980s at the latest.

**Have you always made men's shoes only?**

I started out by learning how to make men's shoes. After striving in that craft for several years, I moved to a different company to learn to make women's shoes. Afterward, I worked for many years making shoes for both sexes. These days, I focus solely on women's shoes, particularly comfort shoes, like sneakers.

**It is natural that the demand for handmade shoes changes over time due to changes in technology and consumer tastes. But don't you miss the heyday**

Yang began making shoes at age 14 alongside an older second
cousin who was working as a shoe patternmaker at the time.
Yang fell in love with this trade at first sight. He says he has
never felt tired of this craft. He is a born shoemaker.

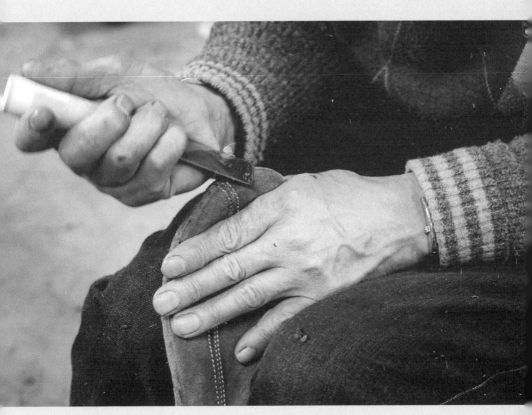

**of your craft?**

I am not sure whether it is even possible to compare shoes made in mass-production factories today to the salon-style handmade shoes we made decades ago. Quality shoes were made in the hands of master craftspeople back then. Today, there are almost no "handmade" shoes to speak of, as the vast majority of shoes on the market are produced in mechanized factories. Comparison is impossible, given the unbridgeable difference in the manufacturing process and techniques.

# 105 Little Steps towards Making a Pair of Handmade Shoes

———

We all dream of wearing a pair of perfectly fitting, comfortable, stylish shoes that have been created only for us. Yet we hesitate to find or order such shoes because we think the price of such specially customized shoes would be too high. Yet Yang begs to differ. He says that we could order and wear a pair of handmade shoes that perfectly fit us for the price we would pay for a pair of typical dress shoes sold at high-end department stores. The price, of course, varies depending on the material, but shoemakers can make you a pair of shoes at the price you want using general leather. Yang wishes that the Handmade Shoe Town would make this possible.

"I wish the shoe town would become a special place that brings together factories and stores. It should have a large parking space so that people could visit here without any hesitation. This area need not be as luxurious and high-end as those fancy shopping malls these days, but it should be a place where consumers in search of quality products can always visit."

**What advantages or benefits do handmade shoes offer that brand-name shoes don't?**

Brand-name shoes are made on the basis of the average sizes of thousands of feet. The usual base is the feet of 1,500 or so people for each standard size. Handmade shoes, on the other hand, are made only for one person's feet.

**Don't craftspeople themselves have the biggest responsibility for reviving this industry?**

Craftspeople are stubborn and extremely individualistic. They have much difficulty mobilizing or joining an order or a system. But their demand is simple: that is, to have a pleasant working environment where they can keep doing what they are good at doing. Before speaking of what roles or responsibilities craftspeople must bear, you need first to understand the psychology of craftspeople. Gather them into a space and talk with them, and you can count on them to make fantastic products insofar as improved working conditions are provided. These days, even cabbage farmers sell their produce under their own names. Why shouldn't shoemakers?

**Isn't the Handmade Shoe Town supposed to serve precisely that demand?**

Well, my fellow tradesmen and I had wished that we had an exhibition space where we could display the samples of creative and innovative shoes we were making before this shoe town came into being. Such a space would have served as a great advertisement for the shoe town, with visitors spreading the news that the upcoming shoe town would display and sell such amazing-looking shoes. This initial process was crucial to us, but the shoe town today is more geared toward selling existing products instead of showcasing real talent and expertizing at work.

**Do you mean that craftspeople need a proper "workshop" more than a**

Before I met and interviewed Yang, I did not know how much hard work and care it took to create a pair of decent shoes. A shoemaker like Yang must visit dozens of stores to find the right materials, use 96 types of intermediary items—including thread, glue and the like—in the shoemaking process, and repeat 105 steps and movements to complete the process.

**store?**

Precisely. We need a space that brings out the best and most innovative attempts from craftspeople. A workshop that combines the production site and the store in one would allow craftspeople to talk with customers while making their products. Customers can see how the products they have ordered are being made and also give valuable feedback.

**Maybe you all need to bring your techniques and designs more up to date in order to revive the shoemaking industry. With such improvements made, consumers will come to think that handmade shoes are better than brand-name ones and help market your products overseas as well.**

We already have world-class skills and techniques. We are able to make shoes as beautiful as those of A. Testoni of Italy. We are capable of making perfect and beautiful shoes according to consumer tastes. Yet we do not—no, cannot—make these good shoes because we are not paid the right price, and consequently cannot use topnotch materials. Italian handmade shoes are famous not necessarily because Italian shoemakers are better skilled, but because they use high quality materials. I think Korean shoemakers are better than their Italian counterparts in terms of skill alone.

**You can make even better shoes so long as you are paid the right prices...**

Yes, and another important thing is time. If we are given enough time, we will spend that much more effort on making and perfecting each pair of shoes we make. Italian shoemakers spend between two days and a week on making a pair of shoes. We, on the other hand, are forced to make a pair in a single day. When we are strapped for time, trying to finish the design, pattern making, fabric cutting and stitching all in one day, how can we produce a masterpiece? Italians also use far advanced machinery than what we use. Machine-wrapping and polishing makes a huge difference to the quality of the finished product.

People should not simply demand the same quality shoes from us when we do not have enough time, money and resources to make them.

**Insofar as shoe companies pay you a fair price and consumers recognize the true value and work that went into making handmade shoes, you could create real quality shoes, couldn't you?**

If things really did happen as you have said, we shoemakers could probably produce the shoes to suit our clients' tastes using even fallen leaves on the street. It is when one has the confidence of being forgiven and able to start anew that one can make various innovative attempts. A masterpiece is often a result of immeasurable trial and error made by failing, but brave, makers. What distinct goods can we produce when we are required to make the same goods over and over for ever decreasing prices? I wish the business environment in Korea were such that people with real skills and expertise could exercise their abilities to the full.

**The most regrettable fact, it seems to me, is that our craftspeople are not able to exercise all their talents and skills to the fullest because of the business environment.**

My guess is that we are showing only about 60 percent of what we could accomplish. We live hand-to-mouth lives, so can seldom think about developing innovative techniques or designs. But that is why the Handmade Shoe Town and other such governmental initiatives should provide real and substantial support for craftspeople to develop innovative products.

Before I met and interviewed Yang, I did not know how much hard work and care it took to create a pair of decent shoes. A shoemaker like Yang must visit dozens of stores to find the right materials, use 96 types of intermediary items — including thread, glue and the like — in the shoemaking process, and repeat

"Look how gorgeous these shoes look, made by really skilled shoemakers. These handmade shoes fundamentally differ from the shoes made by machines in factories. We should revive this amazing technique and trade."

105 steps and movements to complete the process. Yet Yang, along with other craftspeople, warns that one cannot support a family on a shoemaker's income alone. The Handmade Shoe Town, looking sophisticated with its European décor, kept shining brightly at night, cannot dispel the shadow of worries over the future of the shoemaking industry in Korea.

After our interview, Yang and I took a tour of the joint shoe store at the Handmade Shoe Town. Yang searched for and picked up a product from his company from one of the shelves, and said with a confident smile.

"Look how gorgeous these shoes look, made by really skilled shoemakers. These handmade shoes fundamentally differ from the shoes made by machines in factories. We should revive this amazing technique and trade. There will be few in the future to remain in this field and teach and impart their craft to young people. Proper workshops should be set up, whether in the form of a district or a town, so that craftspeople could exercise their skills and ability to the fullest and young people would flock there to learn this amazing trade."

Yang is an expert who is capable of producing beautiful, comfortable shoes with almost any material given him, whether it be fallen leaves, feathers, or even glass. One day, we might have the world's most renowned handmade shoe company, operating out of a tiny, but cozy, workshop at the corner of a street in Seongsu-dong, Seoul.

*I could make shoes even with fallen leaves if people were to recognize the true value of my work.*

# Kim
Sang-sil

—

Master Jewelry Craftsman
25 years of work

# Current Status of Traditional Jewelry Craft in Korea: Excellent Jewelry Makers, Poor Distribution Support

—

| | |
|---|---|
| 1960 | Born in Gochang, Jeollabuk-do. |
| 1991 | Quit job and entered the field of jewelry making. |
| 1993 | Set up a jewelry making factory. |
| 1997 | With the factory in bankruptcy, opened a new fashion accessory store in Namdaemun. |
| 2002 | Began to learn and practice the fashion accessory making craft. |
| 2013 | Became Korea's first government-recognized "master maker" of traditional jewelry and fashion accessories. |
| Present | Runs and teaches at the Traditional Handicraft Modernization Institute. |

We have met with numerous expert makers of apparel, shoes, and bags—objects that are familiar to us and that form part of our daily lives. Fashion accessories and jewelry, on the other hand, and particularly traditional-style accessories and jewelry, do not strike us as items of daily living. Traditional accessories, in particular, remain an exotic subject to us. We should perhaps more appropriately regard these items as part of culture and the arts rather than of manufacturing. Given this difference and novelty of the trade, I went to meet my interviewee for this chapter, Korea's first officially recognized master maker of traditional jewelry Kim Sang-sil, with mounting excitement and curiosity.

The Traditional Handicraft Modernization Institute is quite easy to find and access. The institute is located on the second floor of a building right across from the Chungmu-ro Subway Station, on a main street in the heart of Seoul that attracts millions of international visitors every year. It is at this institute where Kim strives to modernize the unique aesthetics of traditional Korean handicrafts. While Kim was given the official, government-granted title of being a master maker of traditional-style jewelry in 2013, he has been working in this field for 25 years already, with the last 15 spent on fashion accessories and jewelry in particular.

As I expected, the top of his work table in his office sparkled with things rare and beautiful. There were numerous gemstones in their raw forms, including pearls, coral, quartz, jade and crystal. Inside a small box at one corner of the table were various parts and goods Kim needed to make his jewelry, such as tree branches and plastic molds. Some of Kim's finished works were hanging on one wall of the office, boasting a special beauty and an exquisite finish. It is Kim's habit to show some of his finished works to all first-time visitors to his office. He is a craftsman who wants to show his works rather than explain his craft with many words.

*As I expected, the top of his work table in his office sparkled with things rare and beautiful. There were numerous gemstones in their raw forms, including pearls, coral, quartz, jade and crystal.*

# Fashion Jewelry Is a High Value-Added Industry

As I kept admiring his works on site, Kim picked up a tiara that looked bold and glamorous.

"I make a tiara by rolling up the wire first. This allows me to create something that can be bent and shaped as the user sees fit."

All the works Kim creates and designs are characterized by one thing: they all consist of bendable metal wires, onto which Kim places beads and other such decorative materials. Most fashion accessories and jewelry on the market come in fixed shapes. Kim's works therefore provide a very distinctive and flexible alternative.

"This is a technique I found first. I see more and more jewelry makers adopting this technique these days, some of whom I taught myself. A great advantage of fashion jewelry making is that you can create products of almost any design you want, anywhere, so long as you have all the right materials. Most fashion accessories and jewelry come in fixed shapes, but mine can be stretched and bent into an almost infinite variety of shapes."

**This is a necklace that can also serve as a brooch. I love how the pearl is made to look like morning dew on the leaf of a plant. How long does one need to work in this field to become a recognized master like yourself?**

You can't get that kind of title and honor by merely working in this field a long time. You need to participate in a public contest of master craftspeople, organized by the Ministry of Culture, Sports and Tourism (MCST), and pass the evaluation process. The evaluation process was so long and cumbersome! First, you need to have a unique technique of your own in order to be eligible to apply to participate in the process. The entire evaluation process takes a good several months to complete, with the MCST requiring so much paperwork and submissions from you. I had to give them 80 photographs of the things I created for a single portfolio. The document screening process involves five reviewers. Given how laborious this process is, it is no wonder that even people with exquisite skills do not dare rise to the challenge.

**To become a publicly recognized master craftsperson, I guess you need not only to be good at what you do, but also have the perseverance to survive all the paperwork involved.**

The area of Wangsimni in Seoul used to be famous for its mother-of-pearl products. There are few expert mother-of-pearl craftspeople remaining in that town today. The few that remain there are seasoned and skilled experts. Whenever I tell them to apply for the government's evaluation of master craftspeople, though, they shake their heads, saying how could they prepare all the required paperwork at such a late age.

**There is want for more active and systemic support from the government to identify and support talented and skilled craftspeople.**

Yes, there is. The government should realize how important this fashion accessory industry is. They have no idea of the great added value and potential that the fashion jewelry industry can offer. I think it has the best prospects of all the industries existing in Korea.

**How advanced is the fashion jewelry industry in Korea?**

Korea is easily one of the five countries in the world with the largest and best fashion jewelry markets. Korean designers and craftspeople are as capable as their French or Italian counterparts. There is no problem with skills. The problem is in distribution. The status of fashion jewelry distribution is so backward in Korea that we hardly have any brand we could proudly introduce to the world.

*All the works Kim creates and designs are characterized by one thing: they all consist of bendable metal wires, onto which Kim places beads and other such decorative materials. Most fashion accessories and jewelry on the market come in fixed shapes. Kim's works therefore provide a very distinctive and flexible alternative.*

Kim says we can easily see for ourselves how skilled, innovative and advanced our jewelry designers, craftspeople and merchandisers are just by taking a tour of such neighborhoods as Hongdae and Insa-dong. These days, the Namdaemun Market is also emerging as a new center for the Korean fashion accessory industry.

# Namdaemun Market is the Key to the Future of the Korean Fashion Accessory Industry
---

Kim sat up in his chair and the look on his face became more serious as he mentioned the words "Namdaemun Market." He was determined to explain its true importance.

"Namdaemun houses over 6,000 shops that specialize in the wholesale distribution or exporting of fashion accessories. The goods these shops handle are all bulk-produced at factories. Namdaemun is a world-class fashion accessory market. The market offers easy access to raw materials and finished goods alike. That is why merchants come from neighboring countries to Namdaemun in search of quality materials and products. At Namdaemun, you will understand why I say the fashion accessory industry has great potential and needs to be fostered into a key national industry."

**Would you say the fastest and most efficient way to foster the Korean fashion jewelry industry is to support the Namdaemun Market?**

Namdaemun attracts over 3,000 jewelry dealers per day. The market is officially recognized as generating KRW 6.5 trillion in revenue each year. These statistics, however, do not reflect the full potential of the market. Namdaemun bears witness to the infinite prospect that the fashion jewelry industry can offer the Korean economy. We have such a large industry full of potential, yet the size of the domestic market is limited. Almost 70 percent of the products we make are exported abroad. Of the 6,000 wholesale and exporting stores at Namdaemun, 1,000 to 2,000 handle goods imported from China, India and Vietnam, and the remainder deal in goods made in Korea. Forty percent of the goods handled by these stores are designed and produced by Koreans. Korean jewelry designers and craftspeople produce over 2,500 new designs every day. Aren't these figures overwhelming?

**Please tell me more about the characteristics of the fashion accessory industry in Korea.**

The division of labor arose spontaneously in this industry, with distributors first selling at Namdaemun Market and producers and designers flocking to the area later, forming a natural conveyor belt system over time. A designer creates a design, then the molder and caster get to work. Polishing comes in, followed by plating and assembly. There are specialists of all kinds here, including those with expertise attaching stones, packing, and trading overseas. The development and production of intermediary parts mostly take place at factories in Namyangju, Incheon, Seongnam, and Suwon. These parts come together for assembly at Namdaemun, and the finished products are put on display here as well. We makers of finished products are glad to have reliable partners capable of producing quality intermediary parts. This spontaneous division of labor maximizes our efficiency as a whole, and is unseen anywhere else around the world.

**When did the fashion accessory industry in Korea begin to grow so much?**

Ironically, it began when Korea was undergoing the severest economic and financial crisis in its history in the late 1990s. Jewelry factories until then were

*"The government should realize how important this fashion accessory industry is. They have no idea of the great added value and potential that the fashion jewelry industry can offer. I think it has the best prospects of all the industries existing in Korea."*

mostly small-scale, employing three to ten people each. These factories did not need to "restructure" and lay off people at the sudden onset of the economic crisis because people in this business were already efficiently sharing their workloads. As producers of materials and intermediary parts began to take up design themselves, they were able to create quality goods at even cheaper prices, thus attracting bulk orders. That is why the fashion accessory industry grew so large when other industries began to decline.

### How were things in this industry in the 1970s and the 1980s?

In the 1970s, the Korean government set up a major jewelry factory at Iksan in Jeollabuk-do, and followed up with the creation of an industrial cluster specializing in gemstone cutting and processing. It was from then on that the industry began to export over USD 10 million worth of goods overseas. The industrial cluster initially dealt in limestone. As the quality of Korean-made limestone jewelry became recognized worldwide, we began to receive orders for polishing raw diamonds as well. With the change of government, however, the industrial cluster no longer received any public support, forcing an increasing number of skilled craftspeople to move to Seoul in the early 1980s in search of jobs. Some of these craftspeople went to Jongno 3-ga, and others settled in and around Namdaemun and Hoehyeon-dong to create quality jewelry.

### That is how the Namdaemun Market became the center of the fashion accessory industry today.

Yes, it is. The government can therefore foster the fashion accessory industry by supporting Namdaemun Market. It provides an overarching frame and system for the whole industry. Place an order for anything here at Namdaemun, and you will get it within a month at the latest. The market deals in all kinds of goods imported from everywhere worldwide. Until now, it has been perceived as largely operating outside the boundaries of the law, but the government can always encourage the sellers at this market to become legitimate by giving them legal support and benefits. With the range of goods legitimately available at this market widening, it will begin to attract buyers and tourists from all around the world and become a major center of trade in Korea. Many of the goods on offer at Namdaemun are also quality products. The Yiwu Market in China may be larger in absolute size, but Namdaemun offers better quality. The Yiwu Market has grown so large thanks to the Chinese government's support. The market is said to hire all locals in the neighboring towns, and is fast becoming a global center of bag and fashion accessory manufacturing.

# To Become Part of People's Daily Lives: That Is the Goal of Modernizing Traditional Handicrafts

—

Kim explained all these in a calm manner, all the while working on his new project. I was mesmerized by the consistency and speed with which he kept placing tiny beads on a metallic wire. After accumulating much experience in jewelry processing, he even founded and ran a jewelry factory for a number of years.

**Where did you learn this trade?**

There were no schools or programs that provided formal lessons on fashion accessories when I started out. I had to learn all the things I needed to know by myself. While running a jewelry factory, I strove to learn from my employees by glancing at their work all the time. I also visited various factories to learn new and different techniques.

**I hear that you majored in mechanical engineering at college and worked at**

**Korea Communications Corporation before you entered this field. A public corporation of that kind was one of the most admired workplaces in Korea at the time. Why did you quit?**

I got a job with that company because others kept telling me to, saying I would be making a wise choice by working there. Deep in my heart, though, I had always dreamed of making something beautiful with my own hands. When I was little, I made a miniature turtle ship one day, using only a razor blade and a scrap piece of chestnut wood. I did it as homework, but received an award from the superintendent of the provincial Board of Schools for Jeollabuk-do. Both my parents were good with their hands, and many of my family members and relatives were born with very rich, artistic sensibilities. I spent a childhood surrounded by traditional Korean vocal art, Korean flute and percussion music, and calligraphy.

**How were things at first when you entered this field of jewelry making? Didn't you struggle running your own business after working so many years as an office worker?**

Actually, things went quite well for me at first. I started out as an intermediary wholesale distributor, supplying goods from factories to jewelry stores. At first, my main areas were in Incheon and other satellite towns of Seoul, but I eventually succeeded in entering Myeongdong and Namdaemun. To enter these markets, one had to have real quality goods. I also took advantage of the latest marketing techniques at the time, like telemarketing, raffles and celebrity endorsements. My company received an endless stream of orders.

**But then the Asian Financial Crisis occurred.**

Yes, my company grew large enough to require 50 employees. A big company like that was especially vulnerable to the Asian Financial Crisis and its aftermath. After my company went bankrupt, I set up a new fashion accessory shop at Namdaemun and began to focus on creating unique, beautiful things, researching day and night to improve my designs.

**I wonder what made you turn to traditional-style jewelry after running a modern jewelry factory.**

While working on launching a joint brand of 340 jewelry producers located in Namdaemun Market, I had the chance to attend an industrial fair overseas. At the fair, I saw that Korean-made goods surpassed goods from other countries in quality, but were not recognized or given fair treatment as such. This was because the designs of those Korean-made goods, mostly from Namdaemun, were counterfeits of foreign brand jewelry. That was when I realized the importance of having our own brand offering things original to the world.

**Jewelry combining lacquer and mother-of-pearl inlay is your specialty now, isn't it?**

I truly believe that lacquer ware inlaid with mother-of-pearl is a unique Korean contribution to world jewelry design and jewelry making. I wanted to apply this cherished part of traditional Korean handicraft to fashion accessories that people wear on a daily basis. That is what we modernizers of traditional handicrafts aim to achieve. The exquisite patterns on Goryo-period celadon and lacquer ware inlaid with mother-of-pearl are beautiful and proud parts of our heritage, but our job is to bring them out into the real, modern world we inhabit today through modification and adaptation. Insisting on keeping these traditional techniques as they are will enable us only to make some generic tourist souvenirs. We need to actively apply these techniques to objects that we use daily. Look at this hairpin, made of leather and decorated with mother-of-pearl-inlaid lacquer. You have never seen anything like this anywhere else in the world. Look at France. The country has the world's best-known hairpin brand, which now sustains an entire town. Why shouldn't we do something similar in

*"Deep in my heart, though, I had always dreamed of making something beautiful with my own hands."*

Korea? We have creative designers and skilled craftspeople. I took some of my works to China recently, and the Chinese swooned over them in amazement.

**I am glad to see that you continue to innovate. I was particularly impressed by your work showing mother-of-pearl patterns on *hanji* (traditional Korean paper).**

I created that because I wanted to make a brooch that was lighter to wear. These days, I am taking a program at the MCST on the modernization of handicrafts. It has been of great help to me. I have had much to learn from all those renowned designers and craftspeople from across Korea and around the world. I am also taking private lessons on computer-aided design of jewelry. I could outsource the CAD work, but would prefer to do it on my own to my own liking.

**From where do you draw inspiration for new designs?**

For me, design research involves copying the old designs I myself created in the past. I try to improve upon past designs and mistakes one at a time. That is how innovation works, I think. Inspiration does not hit you out of the blue overnight. You have to work at it constantly.

**I hear that you are the only jewelry maker in Korea who makes jewelry by applying traditional handicraft techniques. It must be a solitary path you are walking now. How did you feel when you were recognized by the government as the first and best in your field?**

There are a few masters of lacquer ware inlaid with mother-of-pearl, but I believe I am the first in jewelry making to be recognized formally as such. I am happy that I have helped to broaden the concept of "master craftspeople" in Korea. Before I was given this honor, people kept complaining that the prices of my works were too high. Nowadays, they at least bother to compliment me, saying my works are different because they are created by a master. It is at these moments that I feel proud of the choice I have made.

**Now that you have pioneered this path, there will soon be second and third government-recognized jewelry masters, don't you think?**

I truly hope so. Now that the government has given my craft this kind of recognition and support, hopefully more and more people will be tempted to walk this path.

# Korea Has World-Class Jewelry Craftspeople and Skills: We Now Need Systematic Support for Distribution

———

In March 2013, Kim launched the Seoul Fashion Crafts Cooperative (SFCC), bringing together people interested in combining modern fashion with traditional Korean handicrafts.

"The more I work in this field, the more I come to realize the importance of improving upon and adapting our traditional culture. I am interested in applying traditional handicrafts to dressmaking. I would also like to gather resources with my fellow craftspeople and set up a space that introduces works of traditional handicrafts to international tourists. It will be a high-end store for goods made in Korea, which also entertains visitors with shows and performances. We may also need to set up a wholesale distribution center for Korean-made goods in a major city like Harbin, China so as to market our goods better."

**What are your other hopes and dreams?**

I would like to establish a school to train future generations of craftspeople. I have been teaching classes, but wish I could do it on a more systematic scale. I would like to teach future generations of craftspeople, help them start their own businesses, and also offer diverse classes on how handicrafts may be adapted to modern life. Handicrafts can serve therapeutic purposes. They also make good subjects of public learning programs. Why not include them in the curriculum for elementary schools, for the occupational therapy programs at hospitals, or for lifelong education programs at local district offices and the like?

**Talking with you, I feel that we need to broaden our perspective on fashion accessories and jewelry.**

Did you know that jewelry making used to be categorized as an "antique business" under the old income tax law? In the past, jewelry makers were usually owners of small local watch shops, whose major trade was in fixing and repairing defunct wristwatches while selling gold rings on the side. The law was amended in the mid-1990s, but I am not sure whether the public perception of our trade is as up to date. There are a number of colleges in Korea offering programs on jewelry making, but only one has a program on fashion accessories.

**Hong Kong apparently draws upon its jewelry distribution industry for 11 percent of its gross national product. Do you think the fashion accessory industry needs more policy support to enhance its profitability?**

I do not see any reason why it shouldn't. The government can help us by strengthening the channels of distribution. With systematic distribution, manufacturing will naturally revive. In order to globalize our market, we need support for advertising and marketing our goods as well. The government has a big role to play in this regard.

**Visiting all those industrial fairs and expos abroad, you must compare the Korean situation to the cases of other countries.**

Every time I visit such a show, I think to myself: Why not set up dozens of booths at world-renowned fashion shows to advertise fashion accessories made in Korea? Our goods already are of excellent quality, so they would sell well. If I could just travel around the world for three years and keep advertising goods made in Korea and in Namdaemun to international buyers, I would be a truly happy man.

**What do consumers worldwide think of Korean-made fashion accessories?**

I recently visited an industrial fair in Italy, and cannot forget the buyers there who kept swooning over the beauty and quality of handcrafted goods from Korea. We Koreans may undervalue our own, but buyers worldwide are impressed with what we produce. I was so taken up with their reaction to our goods that I even came away thinking that the future core of the whole Korean culture may be in handicrafts.

**Koreans have been famous for millennia around the world for their exquisite handicrafts.**

Look at our floor-heating system, known as *ondol*. With this ondol culture, we Koreans have been taught from birth on, generation after generation, to sit on heated floors and focus on doing things with our hands. Sitting like that on the floor naturally gives us an unshakable balance, which we could apply to perfecting our handicrafts. Koreans are also perseverant.

**Do you really think the fashion accessory industry holds the key to the future of the Korean economy so long as it is given adequate policy support?**

The United States, Germany and Japan may have bigger markets and better systems in this regard, but I am sure Koreans are among the world's top three nations in terms of technique and skill. With adequate support for distribution, we can easily top the list, and the entire nation can run on the fashion accessory industry. The kind of factories we need do not require any smoke stacks or

"The United States, Germany and Japan may have bigger markets and better systems in this regard, but I am sure Koreans are among the world's top three nations in terms of technique and skill. With adequate support for distribution, we can easily top the list, and the entire nation can run on the fashion accessory industry."

major investments. These factories can be set up anywhere across the nation. Who but Koreans can even attempt to produce fine lacquer ware inlaid with mother-of-pearl? I am sure that I am the best in my field. With this level of expertise and technique, we can easily become top players on the global market. I am ready, as are other craftspeople so far, to take on the world. The government should support us.

Kim has pioneered and walked his path for decades even when others underestimated his innovation. He never complained even when no one gave him any kind words of encouragement and support. He kept making his beautiful products and quietly, but confidently, presented them to the world as indicators of the level of craft and skill in Korean manufacturing.

Toward the end of our interview, Kim finished his wiring work and took a little break before fixing the pin onto the back of the brooch. He remained attentive to the work in his hands at every moment. The kind of dedication he showed toward his craft seemed enough to me to raise our hopes for the future of the Korean fashion accessory industry.

# Resuscitating Dongdaemun with a New R&D Cluster

**Cho Dong-seong (Professor, College of Management, Seoul National University)**

Dongdaemun is the undisputed center of Korea's fashion and apparel industries, with a clothing market that, on a daily basis attracts over 400,000 visitors and generates more than KRW 40 million in sales. In the international fashion industry today, however, the Dongdaemun Market faces growing challenges and dilemmas. The direct inspiration for Dongdaemun is Milan, Italy. Dongdaemun is equipped with an integrated system that completes the production and delivery of goods in 72 hours after receiving photographs of new fashion designs featured at the latest *prêt-à-porter* collections. Leading *prêt-à-porter* shows, along with influential *haute couture* shows, take place in such traditional world capitals of fashion design such as New York City, Milan, and London. Ningbo, a growing town in the Chinese province of Zhejiang, is rumored to have a similar system, but the system is not as advanced or efficient, particularly with respect to logistics and design, as ours in Korea. Yet the Chinese system costs only one-fifth of what ours does, so it will not be long before the Chinese apparel manufacturers catch up.

We continue to rely on Italy and other advanced countries for new designs and inspiration, while the Chinese are close behind us. We cannot and ought not stoop down to the latecomer's level and compete head on with the Chinese in terms of manufacturing cost and efficiency alone. Instead, we ought to discover new ideas and designs. Yet we lack the will and resources to do so. Once the Chinese take over apparel manufacturing from us,

Dongdaemun will instantly turn into a ghost town. In order to ensure the sustainable future and growth of Dongdaemun as Korea's capital of fashion design and apparel, we must develop a clear and systematic plan.

## New Schools for Creative Talent

In 2008, I had the chance to take a research break from my job as a faculty member at a Korean university, and spent that year doing research on the local competitiveness of Korea, along with Professor Michael Porter at Harvard Business School. I decided to approach the required analysis using the cluster theory—namely, how businesses and other organizations, specializing in the same or related functions, come to gather and form a cluster in a given area. Having decided on the apparel industry cluster at Dongdaemun as the main subject of my research, I began to make a comparative analysis of Dongdaemun and the Garment District of New York City.

The key word that sets apart the two seemingly similar towns is diversity. Dongdaemun specializes in apparel production only. The Garment District, on the other hand, is a multi-functional cluster that houses businesses and agencies of diverse specialties, including research and development (R&D) labs and distributors. In the Garment District, fashion is only part of an evolving and expanding web of local fashion design, architecture and art. The district thus includes artistic strongholds like Chelsea, and is also home to the main offices of renowned journalistic publications, including *The New York Times*, *The New Yorker* and *Vanity Fair*.

In order for Dongdaemun to become a multi-functional cluster like the Garment District, it must be capable of attracting businesses involved in all fashion-related specialties, particularly R&D centers and labs specializing in upstream business activities. R&D is the most important and urgently needed element at Dongdaemun, and we can solve this problem by establishing new schools. The fatal weakness of Dongdaemun today is that it lacks a system that educates and develops the next generation of fashion designers and industry leaders. Silicon Valley has become the capital of information technology worldwide thanks to Stanford University. The biotech belt along National Route 128 in and around Boston remains productive and powerful because of the Massachusetts Institute of Technology and Harvard University. The Zhongguancun High-Tech Zone of China similarly thrives thanks to Beijing and Tsinghua Universities.

New ideas and innovations generated on campus inevitably flow into industry. When we do not use our own brains to generate such innovations, we are forced to rely on others' brains. The key impetus that leads an industrial cluster to the next level of growth is the presence of universities capable of performing effective academic-industrial collaboration projects. If we were really intent on developing Dongdaemun into a leading fashion cluster with worldwide influence, we need to establish a new school that can produce the next generation of creative leaders. Once we form a college campus specializing in the next generation of fashion designers and workers in the region, Dongdaemun will naturally develop into a world-class fashion design cluster with ties to the nearby industrial clusters at Cheonggyecheon and Euljiro.

We cannot disregard the significant impact that fashion schools exert on surrounding cities, as illustrated by the likes of Central Saint Martins in London, Parsons School of Design in New York City, and the Royal Academy of Fine Arts in Antwerp. These institutions are not ivory towers detached from real-world concerns, but are the centers of local social and economic life, wielding intellectual leadership over local industries. The fashion shows organized every year by prospective graduates of these schools attract hundreds of thousands of visitors from around the world. These graduates go on to lead the new waves and currents in fashion design worldwide, serving as barometers of the global apparel industry. Schools lead industries and industries provide graduates with jobs and careers. Fashion schools are not just higher learning institutions, but can imbue whole local communities with new energy and inspiration.

Imagine a new fashion school in Dongdaemun, with thousands of students commuting to and from it daily. The school will serve as new lungs for the entire town, injecting into it breaths of new life and creativity. Only with such a reservoir of creativity at its base can we ensure the continued development and innovation of Dongdaemun. In any given country, the central source of creativity are schools, and these schools must be able to present feasible alternatives to the *status quo*. The models we should emulate are not the prestigious universities like Harvard and Yale, but specialized trade schools for the talented and the passionate, such as Parsons and the Fashion Institute of Technology (FIT). With a couple of schools like these, Dongdaemun will soon transform itself into a capital of high fashion.

## The Power of Dongdaemun Derives from the Gigantic Ecosystem of Apparel Production

The former site of the Dongdaemun Stadium has been turned into the Dongdaemun History and Culture Museum and the Dongdaemun Design Plaza — together known as the DDP. Personally, I wished that the site had been turned into a new fashion school campus. I even went on to estimate all the likely benefits of setting up such a school there. A creative campus on this site, with a floor area ratio of 350 percent, would have introduced research facilities that could hire 500 researchers and learning facilities for 1,000 students. It would also have provided the 250,000 local fashion and apparel experts with opportunities to teach their trade. If we assume the respective values of a researcher, a student and a mature student in continuing-education at KRW 150 million, KRW 100 million and KRW 0.5 million, respectively, the campus would have generated KRW 300 billion in new value each year. By continuing the school for three decades, we could have generated KRW 9 trillion in total.

Aside from this directly-generated value,, the new campus would also have raised the added value of the Dongdaemun Fashion Town by 20 percent a year, from the current annual revenue of KRW 14.6 trillion. In other words, the campus would have generated KRW 87 trillion more over a three-decade span in indirect added value. Developing the former Dongdaemun Stadium site into a school campus would have generated at least 11 times more in direct, and 23 times more in indirect value than selling the site to a realtor. The case vividly illustrates the need for policymakers to carefully consider all possible alternatives and options before settling on any development plans.

At other times, I also wonder if it would have been better had the old Dongdaemun Stadium been kept intact. Whenever a major sporting event took place at the Stadium, tens of thousands of people gathered there at once. The Stadium was the spine of public and community life in the area. That central venue of public excitement no longer exists.

There is a growing voice these days that the DDP should be made into a center not for fashion design, but for the entire fashion industry. A fashion district and cluster like Dongdaemun should include establishments in diverse industries and activities in the long run, for diversity will be key to the district's continued vitality. It is questionable, however, whether the Dongdaemun district, in its current form, would survive the process of converging and effectively merging with industries other than those of fashion. For the time being, at least, Dongdaemun should remain the center for fashion design in Korea.

I have strenuously advocated the need to develop an effective R&D system at Dongdaemun, but would also like to emphasize the need to pay attention to the strong advantages that Dongdaemun offers as a cluster for apparel production. The area is home to 250,000 entrepreneurs, designers and dressmakers, working for over 80,000 businesses that make the seamless integration of all related activities — from the production of raw and secondary materials to the distribution of finished products — possible. Dongdaemun, with its ever-evolving and expanding apparel market, is akin to a gigantic coral reef, attracting millions of picky consumers and retailers from Seoul, China, Russia and elsewhere around the world who exert sustained pressure on improving quality and efficiency.

### Dongdaemun as an Example of a Cluster-Centered Economy

I expect the Dongdaemun Cluster to serve as a milestone in the rise and growth of a cluster-centered economy in Korea. In order for this fashion district to retain and enhance its competitiveness, effective partnership is needed between government and businesses. The government ought to provide policies promoting R&D, industry, tax efficiency, environmental preservation and labor protection, while businesses develop mergers and acquisitions, differentiation, products and marketing strategies. The 240 local governments across Korea today have produced one policy after another of developing industrial clusters that will help revive and strengthen the competitiveness of local economies. Given this movement, Dongdaemun has an important role to play as a model industrial cluster for the entire nation to emulate.

Cluster development takes both policy innovation and business strategies. So far, the traditional mold of economic innovation in Korea has been that the government decides policy goals and businesses follow by developing appropriate strategies catering to those goals. From now on, however, the government and business should be equal partners, developing policies and strategies together simultaneously in consultation with each other. That is the only way we can maximize the synergy of government-business partnership.

We have lived through corporation-centered capitalism and society-centered capitalism. Now we are about to enter the era of cluster-centered capitalism. The central focus of the South Korean economy will, accordingly, shift from the few *jaebeol* conglomerates today to tens of thousands of clusters gathering companies of various sizes in the future.

South Korea is the subject of amazement and envy around the world. In July 2013, I was invited by the European Parliament to give a keynote address on the re-industrialization of Europe. In the speech, I focused on what Korea could learn from its competitors in Europe. After the speech, though, I received far more inquiries and interest from the members of the Parliament than I expected. What explains this heated interest in Korea? It reflects the European belief that Europe lost its position to Korea. Europe used to be the traditional stronghold for electronics, automobiles, and shipbuilding, all of which are now the specialties of Korean industries.

Korea also invests four percent, or the second-largest percentage share of its GDP, in research and development. Korea used to be third in the world in this regard, after Sweden and Israel, but soon caught up with Israel. In terms of the number of patent applications filed worldwide, Korea used to rank fourth in a lineup that included the United States, Japan and Germany, but has recently beat Germany in a lineup that now includes the United States, China, Japan and Korea.

Milan and Paris today must be wary of Dongdaemun's strength and rise. These European cities have already lost much of their influence and strength as fashion capitals of the world to New York City, and Seoul is now emerging as another potential rival. The country of "Gangnam Style," a country that heavily invests in research and development, and an emerging power of cultural and pop content, Korea effectively threatens the established world's leadership over fashion, culture and the arts.

The world's fear of us indicates the strength of our underdeveloped potential. Every now and then, I take a night trip to the Dongdaemun Fashion Town. The shopping mall bustles with even more people and endless rows of neon signs at night than during the day. Every time I make such a visit, I cannot help but get excited over the expanding and evolving apparel industry cluster to be established at Dongdaemun, attracting young and creative talent.

**About Cho Dong-seong**
Cho graduated from Seoul National University with a bachelor's degree in business administration in 1971. He went on to receive his doctorate from Harvard Business School in 1977. After working at the Boston Consulting Group and Gulf Oil, he began teaching at Seoul National University in 1978. Ever since, he has been researching and teaching subjects on management strategy, international management, management innovation and design management. In 2009, Cho was ranked third among the 30 most influential business gurus in Korea, and also was the highest-ranked career academic (*Maeil Gyeongje Economy*). An author of the "M" theory (that successful and long-surviving businesses have their own mechanisms), Cho is a source of inspiration and wisdom for many CEOs struggling with today's recession-prone economy. Trusted worldwide, Cho also became the first Korean to host a session at a recent World Economic Forum at Davos.

# Three Steps toward Making Dongdaemun a Central Hub for Fashion Industries in Asia

**Park Hun (Researcher, Korea Institute for Industrial Economics and Trade)**

The total value of fashion and apparel industries in Korea amounts to KRW 40 trillion, almost 13.5 percent of the entire domestic market and much larger than the value contributed by automobiles or electronics. Almost 2.5 million people, including wholesale and retail distributors as well as tourists, visit Dongdaemun from outside Korea every year, purchasing KRW 13 trillion-worth of apparel goods. All these figures are from a statistical report released in 2011, and remain on a steady rise. Dongdaemun is still a must-see destination for countless international tourists. Unfortunately, however, Chinese wholesale and retail distributors—Dongdaemun's major clients—are deserting Dongdaemun. Why? Not far from the industrial town of Ningbo in China is the Yiwu Market, home to thousands of local craftspeople and small vendors. The market, almost 10 times larger than Dongdaemun, features all goods of light manufacturing one could possibly imagine, including toys and fashion accessories. Clothing has its own sizable section in the market. Goods featured here are not of any noteworthy quality, but are incredibly cheap. Korean-made goods may be a little better in quality, but not dramatically. As Korean-made goods sold at Dongdaemun mostly lack the "Made in Korea" labels, it is nearly impossible to prove that they were indeed made in Korea. That is why Chinese buyers buy less and less from Dongdaemun. We should now ask how we might improve the system at Dongdaemun to bring these Chinese clients back.

## Solution 1: Fashion Designers at Dongdaemun

Koreans used to say that everything can be found in Dongdaemun. Yet the market lacks two of the most crucial elements: namely, brands and designers. The absence of fashion designers means that there is little role that fashion designers can play in the current system. Much of the business in Dongdaemun, in other words, is centered on wholesale and retail distributors.

Dongdaemun is a market of subcontractors through and through that operates all its processes according to wholesale distributors' orders. That is why the district specializes in making low-end goods. Wholesale distributors never order high-end. The prime value for them is affordability. Fashion designers who insist on original artistic vision are only superfluous to the entire process. Original designs and brands are luxuries that this market cannot afford. This is a matter of structure and system and not of individuals. The system places designers near the bottom of the endless chain of subcontracts.

This problem has long plagued Dongdaemun. Any solution would require conscious and concerted effort from all parties. Designers and wholesale distributors need to work together with genuine commitment to achieving substantial change. One of the main strengths of New York City as a world fashion capital is that the city is home to creative and original designers, both well-established and up-and-coming. The fashion industry in New York City is centered on designers and not on distributors. The New York fashion market may be shrinking in size somewhat, but still exerts far-reaching influence worldwide. The case is exactly the opposite in Korea. Here designers can hardly lead and order the production process, with the majority of businesses content in producing low-end goods that generate easy money. Designers and industry specialists with an eye for original design tend to avoid Dongdaemun because they know their insistence on doing things their way will fall on the deaf ears of the established wholesale distributors.

Here is where the role of the government becomes important. The government should devise policy measures to discover, encourage and support Korea's original and struggling fashion brands. In order for Dongdaemun to thrive in the long run, it must support and produce its own designers by providing them with grounds upon which they can exercise their creativity to the fullest extent. A prototype development center is a good example of the kind of resources the government can help create.

The production of a unique item of clothing involves significant trial and error with sample making. Making a pattern sample, however, costs about KRW 300,000 today. Up-and-coming fashion designers cannot make hit items without enough financial support. The absence of financial support for sample pattern making is usually high on the list of obstacles that antagonize independent designers. Public support for these and other activities of creative fashion design will therefore prove to be of much help.

### Solution 2: Free Schools for Talented Dressmakers

Koreans are renowned worldwide for their talent at handicrafts and other activities that require attention to detail. Korean apparel manufacturers enjoy popularity worldwide as a result. Yet the dressmaking industry in Korea is in decline. Dressmakers working in and around Dongdaemun today used to be famous for their skills and craft, but the products they make now are not of the same quality because these dressmakers are used to a system that values cheap labor. Give pieces of high-end fabric to dressmakers at Dongdaemun today, and they will mostly fear what they should do with such fabric. Different fabrics require different needles and thread. Seasoned dressmakers would know which needles and thread to use with which fabric, but the majority of dressmakers at Dongdaemun today lack experience with such a wide range of fabric. Therefore they fear novelty. That is why they need re-training, just as employees at corporations regularly receive re-training.

Will dressmakers at Dongdaemun take the re-training programs at their own expense? Not a chance. Even if the government were to provide these schools and programs free of charge, it would take extra effort to make dressmakers come to them, for dressmakers are forced to handle large workloads to earn a subsistence income. The government should therefore provide not only free education, but also grants for taking the re-training programs, in order to encourage dressmakers to learn and improve their skills.

An organization like a dressmaking craft foundation would be indispensable to ensuring the long-term stability of this re-training. Such a foundation would help provide free classes and programs and also ensure greater financial stability, while ensuring even development of different and related dressmaking crafts at Dongdaemun. A designer may produce the most unique and beautiful design in the world, but a patternmaker of insufficient understanding and skill could undermine that uniqueness and beauty. Both the designer and the patternmaker working on a given item of clothing may be knowledgeable and skillful, but the sample maker working next to them, or the dressmaker after them, lacking comparable knowledge and skills, may mangle the entire project. A piece of fine quality clothing can come about only when all parties involved in its design and production possess comparable skills and competency.

Once dressmakers at Dongdaemun are re-trained, they will no longer have to struggle to find new orders. We could bring all the orders we have outsourced back to Dongdaemun. Just as dressmakers want to continue to work, apparel companies also want stable and reliable dressmakers with whom they can work for the long term. In Korea, however, there are few factories capable of processing large-scale apparel orders at the desired levels of competency and reliability. That is why apparel companies complain that they are forced to relocate to China and Vietnam. That the price of labor in Korea is relatively higher than in these emerging countries is only half-true. The average monthly wage for workers in manufacturing in Korea is KRW 3 million, but most dressmakers in Korea make less than half of that. Yet apparel companies complain that dressmaking labor in Korea is expensive because these companies speak of values relative to productivity instead of absolute prices. If Korean dressmakers keep producing clothes that are as low quality as those made by their Chinese or Vietnamese counterparts, why should apparel companies keep hiring and paying Korean dressmakers higher wages? If, however, Korean dressmakers can improve the quality of the goods they produce significantly, they can demand higher wages. Numerous dressmakers in Korea do in fact possess great skill, but the prevailing perception in Korea is that dressmaking is still a relatively simple craft that need not be valued so highly.

### Solution 3: A New Culture for Dongdaemun

There is no unique culture specific to Dongdaemun. Dongdaemun is still a huge mass of markets and shops. Dongdaemun offers goods for the price written on the tag, but there are few other reasons, besides buying something, to visit Dongdaemun. In order to see the area thrive and prosper in the long run, it will be crucial to persuade consumers that Dongdaemun is a place not just to buy goods, but also to have fun. Fashion festivals and galleries that exhibit local designers' works would increasingly attract people, particularly foreign buyers, as well as wholesale and retail distributors. The attention from these potential clients, in turn, will also help local designers improve their designs. Dongdaemun at present, however, fails to provide such a seamless bridge between culture and commerce. A "Dongdaemun culture" can be an impetus to improve the quality of designs and products produced there. Local designers produce quality designs and clothes. Wholesale distributors buy those clothes and distribute them to end consumers. End consumers enjoy these clothes and support the designers, and wholesale distributors will be again encouraged to distribute items of unique and original design. Dongdaemun can and should foster such a virtuous cycle of culture and commerce. It is a wholesale distribution market. It has a sizable and growing retail section, but it has always been and should remain a wholesale distribution market. It should be the first source for dealing in clothes for consumers nationwide. The government therefore has an important role to play in this regard as well: namely, to foster and support collaboration between wholesale distributors and designers.

Ensuring even quality is also necessary. It is important to give international buyers the belief that they can always find clothing items of certain quality in Korea. Policymakers should focus on Dongdaemun because Dongdaemun is the central and leading venue of apparel production today. Their focus should be on how to turn the area into a central hub of fashion industries in Asia. Leaving Dongdaemun as it is today will not guarantee the future of the Korean fashion industry, which is already shrinking for domestic companies due to the expansion of global SPA brands. We can no longer afford to sit idly by as our fashion and apparel industries, generating 85 percent of their income from the domestic market alone, are increasingly forced out by global brands.

## Do Not Underestimate the Potential of the Korean Fashion Market

The Korean fashion market still harbors much untouched potential. Asian consumers still praise Korea and Dongdaemun for the abundance of cheap, quality and even unique clothing items they offer. Koreans may like to denigrate Dongdaemun as a market for cheap counterfeits, but consumers elsewhere beg to differ. Unless we seize the moment and take action now, we are unlikely to make any major attempt to revamp Dongdaemun in the future. Merchants at Dongdaemun should also begin to sell their goods at fixed prices. Korean consumers and travelers hesitate to buy clothes from China not necessarily because the quality is bad, but because they do not know how much of the price is negotiable. Institutional settings and infrastructure matter as much to consumer confidence as does quality.

For now, we may like to believe that it will be impossible to make "Made in Korea" synonymous with quality clothing. With determination, however, there is always a way. We need to awaken the undeveloped potential of our own industries and surprise the world. That is the beginning of a creative economy.

**About Park Hun**

Perceived as a studious researcher of the Korean fashion and apparel industries and also as the most honest and perceptive observer of the relative position of the dressmaking industry in Korea's overall industrial structure, Park currently heads the Materials and Living-Friendly Industries Research Team at the Korea Institute for Industrial Economics and Trade (KIET). In 1991, Park began working at the KIET, a research arm of the Ministry of Industry specializing in microeconomic policies on industries, and has been heading his team for more than a decade. His research interests extend throughout fashion and apparel production, including the development of new materials, the production and distribution of clothing items, and even fashion trends and vogues.

—

# CHAPTER 3

# Crafts contained the breath of their makers will be forever

# Han Sang-min

—

"Total" Dressmaker
38 years of work

# By Teaching Aspiring Dressmakers, I Realized That I Was the Only One Who Refused to See the True Value of My Work

—

| | |
|---|---|
| 1965 | Born in Yeonggwang, Jeollanam-do. |
| 1978 | Entered the world of tailoring and dressmaking as the youngest apprentice at a tailor shop in Gwangju, at age 17. |
| 1983 | Became a "sewing machine master" at age 22. |
| 2006 | Joined the Korea Academy of Fashion and Sewing (KAFS) as an instructor. |
| 2009 | Founded Han Apparel Company. |
| 2013 | Passed the high school diploma qualification examination and became a freshman in the home economics program at Korea National Open University. |
| Present | Continues to run Han Apparel and the Sewing Trade Training Institute, while also serving as the President of the Instructors' Association at the KAFS and as a referee on the government sewing expert licensing evaluations, and studying at university. |

Have you heard the term, "total tailor" or "total dressmaker"? It is definitely not a household term, but it is commonly used in the apparel industry. The industry divides its craftspeople into three categories: unit makers, part makers, and "total" makers. Unit makers specialize in making only one specific part of a garment, such as the cuffs of a dress shirt. A total maker, on the other hand, is capable of making an entire garment from beginning to end.

There is a clear gap in the level of skill of, and treatment accorded to, unit/part makers and total makers. It matters to dressmakers and tailors by learning which specialty they started out in their careers, and on which specialty or specialties they have focused over the years. One could become the most expert at making the cuffs of dress shirts after years of practice, but it would still be nearly impossible for that person to create an entire garment on his or her own. That is why unit makers, after years of accumulating expertise, still have difficulty starting out on their own. Total makers, on the other hand, have much greater choice over the course of their career development.

It was at a small and cozy workshop along the banks of the Cheonggye Stream that I interviewed the subject for this chapter, who had no qualms in describing himself as a "total" maker. The man's name is Han Sang-min, and he has 38 years of work experience behind him. When I visited him at his work for our interview, the first thing that caught my eye was countless layers of dress patterns piled up as high as the ceiling. There were also fabrics of diverse materials and colors on his wide desk. Han was working on making samples for a fashion show at the time.

# How Something Feels at My Fingertips Gives Me Much Information about It

—

Having worked long in fashion, Han comes across as a man who knows how to style himself according to the latest trend. He looks significantly younger than his age. Some first-time customers question whether he really has the 38 years of work experience he claims to.

"I probably belong to the youngest segment of seasoned and expert tailors and dressmakers in Korea. We dressmakers start out on our career at a much younger age than people in other trades. I began working in this field when I was still a teenager. It was common for members of my generation to take up a trade and learn it as soon as they could."

**Are you really capable of making all kinds of garments?**

I can make all kinds of clothes, but I specialize in women's clothing. I make all items of women's clothing, including jackets and blazers, skirts, trousers, and blouses. Everything except T-shirts.

**Do you have your own factory?**

Back in 2009, I started an apparel manufacturing company named Han Apparel. The company produces clothing designed and patterned by company designers, including myself, but we mostly produce goods ordered by other companies and clients. Prior to starting my own business, I worked in the sample-making and development departments of major apparel companies in Korea, designing and making samples for such well-known women's fashion brands as Cresson, Time, Michaa, Objet, and Bando Fashion. My extensive experience with a wide range of garment samples is a huge asset in this line of work. I am confident that I am probably among the best dressmakers in Korea

It was at a small and cozy workshop along the banks of the Cheonggye Stream that I interviewed the subject for this chapter, who had no qualms in describing himself as a "total" maker. The man's name is Han Sang-min, and he has 38 years of work experience behind him. When I visited him at his work for our interview, the first thing that caught my eye was countless layers of dress patterns piled up as high as the ceiling. There were also fabrics of diverse materials and colors on his wide desk.

in terms of the ability to apply new and diverse techniques.

**How do consumers evaluate your clothes?**

I get favorable responses almost all the time. That is because I let my clients explain to me what they want with as much detail as possible before I start on producing the ordered goods. I do my best to make all my samples as true as possible to client specifications and show them to other dressmakers I hire. I also try to give them instructions that are as detailed as possible, explaining down to a single stitch line as to how it should be done. Skilled dressmakers instantly catch what I want by looking at my samples. This ability to communicate and understand is a key indicator of dressmakers' expertise and trustworthiness.

**I wonder how good the clothes are that are made in the process you have just described. Do the finished products satisfy your instructions and expectations?**

Garments are unlike metallic molds or electronic gadgets, and can significantly vary in quality depending on the materials and dressmakers involved. Many fabrics become easily deformed by heat and other such factors. Perfection is an ideal impossible to attain, but we strive to reach that ideal every single day. The clothes we design and make never come out perfectly true to the measurements we wrote on the drawings. We insert seams and use tapes here and there, which lead to fine crinkles that distort the sizes. It also takes time to make and finish luxurious clothing. These days, factories are run so busily that they develop and produce multiple items in a matter of just a week. The entire process, spanning from development to distribution, is so expedited that we dressmakers can hardly spend much time on perfecting a seemingly finished item. There is fierce competition over time and price.

**But I have heard that you have an unusual rule against working past eight o'clock at night. Isn't it common for apparel factories in and around**

**Changshin-dong to operate their sewing machines to nine or 10 o'clock or even past midnight?**

I abide by that rule because I have realized that I become ineffective at managing and monitoring the production process at my company when I am tired. But that "no work past eight" rule is a compromise. Originally, I wanted to run my business for only five days a week, taking the entire weekend off. But that was unrealistic.

**You seem to have a sense of style and an eye for fashion. How did you come to settle in this field? Were you good at doing things with your hands as a child? Did you have specific goals you wanted to achieve when you entered this field?**

I happened upon this trade when I was 17 years old. At the time, I had no choice. I could not afford to learn what aptitudes I had and which career field would best suit me. I needed to find work that would earn me some money. Even before entering this trade, I had worked in all kinds of part-time jobs one could imagine. My father passed away when I was little, so it fell on me to grow fast and support my family. I entered dressmaking because I had heard that this craft could generate a lot of income and feed an entire family easily.

**But you didn't make all the money you needed at first, did you?**

Needless to say, no. I started out as the youngest apprentice at a tailor shop. My first job was to buy all the supplies needed, such as buttons and fabric for linings. These days, this kind of job is done by aspiring designers with college degrees, but things were different back then. Anyway, this seemingly menial job taught me a lot, particularly with respect to what supplies are needed for creating which kinds of garments. After spending half a year or so on running such errands, they let me start hand-stitching. It is only after mastering these tasks of *madome* — hand-stitching the bottoms of garments, sewing on

*"I also try to give them instructions that are as detailed as possible, explaining down to a single stitch line as to how it should be done. Skilled dressmakers instantly catch what I want by looking at my samples. This ability to communicate and understand is a key indicator of dressmakers' expertise and trustworthiness."*

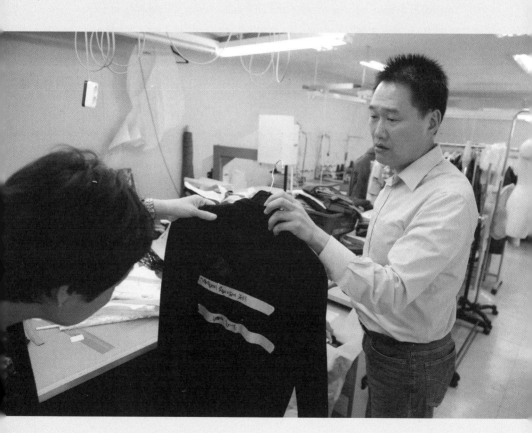

buttons, and making button holes — that one could transition into a *shida*, or an assistant for sewing machine operators. The *shida*'s job includes ironing out garments and cleaning the areas around the seams so that sewing machine operators can do their job. After years of learning one's craft like that, one could finally sit before a sewing machine. Sewing machine operators are accorded much more respect and even called "teachers." Afterward, you learn to make your own patterns and cut your own fabrics. By then you have enough skills to start your own business.

**How long did it take people in your generation to get to that level?**

It usually took people at least a decade. It is while working as a *shida*, ironing and folding fabrics, that I naturally learned how garments were to be sewn. Being a *shida* means you have to learn your craft with your fingertips. I keep telling my students that their fingertips can give them much more information about the materials they are handling than they think. My more than three decades of expertise come from these fingertips of mine.

Han's face began to brighten up as he talked about teaching and his students. He is a passionate instructor at the Korea Academy of Fashion and Sewing.

# By Teaching,
# I Understood the Meaning of Learning
—

Suda Gongbang, a workshop for women created by the True Women's Welfare Shelter at Changshin-dong, opened its doors to the public in 2006. I was the head of the workshop at the time, and transformed it into the Dongdaemun

Fashion Craft School later to provide opportunities for tailors and dressmakers to upgrade their skills. The school was open to everyone interested in learning the dressmaking craft, but its programs particularly focused on people who were already working in the field. The school offered programs at four different levels of difficulty, proceeding from beginner level to intermediate, advanced, and intensive. The school opened as the Korea Academy of Fashion and Sewing, accredited by the Ministry of Knowledge Economy, in 2010.

Han has been with this school since its very beginning. He began working there in August 2006, two months after its opening, and has spent a full decade there. He believes he has been called to teach at the Academy because he has lived more than three decades as a hardworking dressmaker. He is not wrong. He was recruited to the school because he was the most experienced and best qualified of all the candidates.

"At first, I was so nervous and shy that I couldn't even pronounce my name correctly. All the trainees in my class were women. I was known as an expert in my field, but teaching was an entirely different experience. I mumbled and fumbled the first several classes, struggling to speak, give an organized lecture, and help my students with their practice all at once. I continue to struggle to this day, but seem to have improved a lot over the years as a teacher."

**Do you remember any of your first students from 10 years ago?**

At first, I taught an intensive class of 15. Most of the students in that class were part or unit makers who were aspiring to becoming total makers. They were all older than me, with at least three decades of work experience behind them. I was assigned to teach the highest-level class because I had been working in high fashion as a total maker for years. It was these 15 students who later recommended me to the workshop, saying they could learn everything with me, that made me become a full-time teacher. I have taught classes at all four

"Most importantly, it has changed who I am. It has given me a new perspective
on my craft and career. At first, I could not understand why people who were
better educated and smarter than me would come to my class to learn something
from me. I learned this craft solely in order to earn an income for my family.
Their passion for learning moved me greatly, but also filled me with wonder as
to what could drive people to dedicate themselves so much to learning itself.
It was then that I realized this: that I was the only one who refused to recognize
the true value of my own skills."

levels, and learned as much from students as I have taught them.

**You have worked as a full-time teacher for four years already, and still give classes.**

Yes, I do. These days, I mostly teach intensive-level classes. We are in a particularly busy season now, as my students and I have to prepare for the year-end fashion show that has become a tradition at the Academy. I have been blessed to get to know the Academy. I am grateful for being given this opportunity to share my knowledge with others.

**What does it matter so much to you to teach at the Academy?**

Most importantly, because it has changed who I am. It has given me a new perspective on my craft and career. At first, I could not understand why people who were better educated and smarter than me would come to my class to learn something from me. I learned this craft solely in order to earn an income for my family. Their passion for learning moved me greatly, but also filled me with wonder as to what could drive people to dedicate themselves so much to learning itself. It was then that I realized this: that I was the only one who refused to recognize the true value of my own skills.

**I hear that you are taking classes at Korea National Open University yourself these days.**

Yes, I became a freshman in the Department of Apparel at KNOU in 2013 because I thought I could make further progress in my career by combining my practice and expertise with theoretical knowledge. Apparel is my lifelong subject, so I would like to perfect my apparel making craft in a systematic manner. In the field, we dressmakers mostly rely on our intuition and physical perception to make clothes. Now I would like to study and learn which materials would make any given garment. But it is not so easy to work full time and study at the same time. I get dizzy and frantic from time to time, struggling with both goals. At times I feel overburdened, but things are still manageable for me. Now I understand the meaning of learning by teaching. This has been the biggest change for me.

Han passed his high school diploma qualification examination in May 2013. To get to that point, he woke up at four o'clock every morning to find some time to study. Getting up early had been part of his daily life ever since he was a young bachelor, but he had to get up an hour earlier than normal to prepare for his examination. Thanks to this hard work, though, he passed the examination the first time, and without much difficulty.

# Our Tear-Sown Path

——

People working in the apparel industry are officially and publicly recognized as having played a central role in Korea's astonishing economic development and industrialization. Korean dressmakers and tailors are highly praised worldwide for their hard work and skills. Whenever Dov Charney, founder and former CEO of the global apparel corporation American Apparel, recounts his story, he never forgets to mention the two Korean tailors who helped him achieve so much success. Charney founded American Apparel and moved to Los Angeles in 1989, and the Korean dressmakers and tailors in the city met every order on time, no matter how soon the deadlines. Their collaboration worked so effectively that an ad made for the company around this time even bore the words, "Clothes Made by One Jew and Two Koreans."

Yet dressmakers and tailors are hardly accorded the respect, treatment and reward they deserve in Korean society. Han cannot help but lament this current situation.

"Dressmaking is a trade that takes significantly longer for participants to learn and master than other trades. It is that difficult to create and perfect decent pieces of clothing. It may take a bit shorter to become a good part or unit maker, but it definitely takes decades to become a skilled total maker. First, we have to get familiar with and understand all these different clothing styles and materials, and also practice different styles of stitching for thousands of hours to finally become able to create the silhouettes we want. Chiffon and silk, for example, are extremely delicate materials that require extra care when stitching. People who have travelled around the world tell me that, in other countries, even sewing machine operators are treated and respected as designers. That is natural. Work in this field for years, and you will know why dressmakers, tailors and seamstresses should be treated as designers as well."

**Yes, but they still continue to work in dire work environments.**

Our career path is sown with countless tears. I am sure there are people who work hard in environments no better than ours. Even when I try to put my and fellow dressmakers' experience into perspective, though, this feeling of alienation never goes away because we are still not treated as fairly as we deserve. The apparel industry played a crucial role in the economic development of Korea throughout the 1970s and 1980s, but the Korean government today concentrates its attention on information technology only. The industrial structure in Korea is too unjustly biased. People working in other industries can expect their annual wages and bonuses to go up over the years. We dressmakers cannot. Few of us working in this field are given the four mandatory insurance policies or guaranteed retirement benefits. Even the seasoned and skilled ones with decades of work experience behind them have to struggle with meager incomes of barely KRW 1.5 million or 2 million a month. Few apparel companies or factories ever abide by the basic labor law. This fashion and apparel industry still remains in the blind spot of laws and institutions.

**Yes, and you are still paid quite poorly for the orders you process, aren't you?**

There are between 2,000 and 3,000 apparel production factories in the Dongdaemun area alone. These businesses all compete fiercely for the dwindling number of orders by offering impossibly low fees and prices. They engage in this deadly race because they still live desperately hand to mouth. For wholesale distributors, an increase of KRW 500 or KRW 1,000 per garment can amount to a huge difference. Selling 100 T-shirts that cost KRW 500 more each could lead to a loss of KRW 50,000 a day, which is about the daily income for a seamstress.

**I guess that is why you all have your hopes up for the new craftspeople law.**

Yes, we do. I have been noticing for years how the presence of the Academy has ushered in new energy and vitality to the Dongdaemun area. New legislation can exert an even bigger impact. When the legislation finally passed in the National Assembly, I could not help but shed a tear, as it seemed to me that the government was finally recognizing our work.

**You know that people in the apparel industry must work hard themselves first to achieve true reform, don't you?**

That is why an increasing number of us are breaking away from old customs and practices, for example, by going official and registering our businesses. We do not want the government to dole out free gifts and money. We know we have to present an alternative business model ourselves before asking for help. I regret that we have been neglected so much because we ourselves have failed to unite and raise our voice together.

"Our career path is sown with countless tears. I am sure there are people who work hard in environments no better than ours. Even when I try to put my and fellow dressmakers' experience into perspective, though, this feeling of alienation never goes away because we are still not treated as fairly as we deserve."

**What specific hopes do you have regarding the new craftspeople law?**

I sincerely hope that the new law will help ease our financial difficulties. For now, I want nothing more than low-interest loans from the government for manufacturers like us, who have skills to produce high value-added goods, but not enough capital. We cannot apply for loans from banks because our income is irregular throughout the year. The government should help us by providing us with reliable sources of capital so that we can maintain our business operations. Then there is the problem of dire physical working conditions. Our working spaces are usually filled with the strong odor of glue, and mostly located underground. I wish the government would help us create apartment-type factories where skilled people could work in greater comfort. The government could also help us by creating a space where people with quality skills can gather together and create things that boast the uncompromising beauty and quality of Korean products. Finally, we need support so that the training programs taught by experts will also help trainees land jobs more easily.

## We Cannot Focus on Our Work When We Have to Worry Endlessly about Putting Food on Our Table

———

Han takes great pride in his skills and craft. I asked him to compare, as honestly as possible, the clothes made in Italy and in Dongdaemun in Korea. He lowered his voice as he began to answer.

"The fabrics are different, but I think the most significant difference is in the attitude that apparel companies take toward craftspeople. In Korea, apparel companies try to have their orders produced as cheaply as possible, producing thousands of garments of similar materials and similar counterfeit designs. This practice continues to unsettle the entire market order. Few consumers highly value such cheaply made clothes of generic designs. As far as dressmaking skill goes, we Koreans do not lag behind our Italian counterparts. I am certain that Koreans are among the best dressmakers and tailors in the world. Even Italian fashion brands produce most of their goods via overseas manufacturers."

**Are you saying the difference is ultimately a matter of system?**

Look at the clothes made by Korea's famous fashion designers. All those clothes are made by Korean craftspeople. When we have the right working environment where we can focus all our attention and skill on the garments themselves, we can create clothes as good as those from Italy and France. In reality, though, we Koreans have to produce 10 garments a day to put food on our tables, while our Italian counterparts can get by just making three. So how can we be expected to focus on and devote ourselves to each garment we make as much as Italians?

**Are you saying we can improve the quality of clothes produced in Korea by allowing apparel workers to work without worrying about financial issues?**

Precisely. How can we focus on our work when we have to worry endlessly about putting food on our tables? People keep praising the *balli-balli* system of Dongdaemun, amazed at how quickly the factories here are able to process their orders. To me, that seems to be the central problem. We will not achieve significant improvements in either the quality of clothes we make or the quality of our lives unless we first break that system.

**I know Korean dressmakers are praised around the world for their skills, but what about Korean fashion designers?**

*"How can we focus on our work when we have to worry endlessly about putting food on our tables? People keep praising the balli-balli system of Dongdaemun, amazed at how quickly the factories here are able to process their orders. To me, that seems to be the central problem. We will not achieve significant improvements in either the quality of clothes we make or the quality of our lives unless we first break that system."*

I am not sure. Honestly, I think copying rather than creativity is the norm in Korean fashion design. Korea is as notorious as China for its counterfeit goods. We have an increasing number of young aspiring designers who have studied in the United States, Italy, France and such, but apparel companies in Korea rarely hire them. These companies prefer to survey the trends at Dongdaemun Market and copy the most popular designs. This is because fashion companies in this country care only about profit, and not about either quality or customer satisfaction. Even small and medium businesses in this industry do the same because, by copying already popular designs, they can minimize their costs and production times.

**Wouldn't you say the entire Korean society needs to change its perception of the apparel industry and its workers?**

I worry that there will be no dressmakers after our generation. Things are much different for apparel workers in France, Italy, the United States, England and the like. There, skilled apparel workers can enjoy stable occupations and a high quality of life. I am not sure whether we Korean dressmakers would be accorded the same treatment even if Korea were to become a richer nation. We are professionals at what we do, but rarely treated as such, both the market and the government. As you know well, dressmaking or tailoring is a hands-only process. Our trade is not open to automation and machinery. Fabrics and clothes-making techniques evolve every year, and apparel making requires an eye to detail and also the ability to apply and adapt.

**Don't you regret having chosen this path?**

I don't, for one simple reason. It is that I can continue to work in this field even in my old age as long as I am healthy. I believe that learning a trade and mastering the required skills is the best preparation one can make for old age. I plan to work until I am 70 years old. That is why I try to remain in shape

"I don't regret having chosen this path for one simple reason. It is that I can continue to work in this field even in my old age as long as I am healthy. I believe that learning a trade and mastering the required skills is the best preparation one can make for old age. And I am sure there will be roles that I can play in my field as a total maker."

and eat healthy so that I can continue to work. My work may not afford me as much security or income as the civil service or other flourishing businesses do, but I am sure there will be roles that I can play in my field as a total maker.

Han's workspace was exceptionally wider, cleaner and better-lit than some of the other sweatshop-like factories I had visited. Han has already achieved his dream of working in a clean and pleasant work environment. He still finds the rent too high, but hopes he can continue to work in that space for as long as possible. But he understands why other fellow craftspeople cannot do the same.

"Our job involves creating a lot of dust. Office buildings with elevators refuse to rent us tailors and dressmakers space because of the dust. Winter clothing, such as cashmere or woolen coats, is particularly prone to dust. Look how dusty this surface is already!"

He wiped the top of the table standing before him to show me the dust that had accumulated. It reminded me of the dust floating in the air that I saw at a sweatshop in one corner of the Pyeonghwa Market when I was a young factory girl. These sweatshops were so prone to dust that we could hardly see the sunlight through the window because of the dust floating in the air. I wondered now whether the thick layer of fabric fibers characterizing these factories had grown thinner over the years. Efforts to improve the working environment for apparel workers seem to be bearing fruit after fruit, albeit slowly. I am glad to see, anyway, that an increasing number of apparel workers are taking pride in their trade. Han swiftly turned around to face his cutting board. He was eager to finish the dress he was making for the fashion show.

*By teaching aspiring dressmakers,*
*I realized that I was the only one*
*who refused to see*
*the true value of my work.*

# Kim
# Eui-gon

—

Master Tailor
57 years of work

# Learning the Lessons of Tailored Suits from a Silver-Haired Master

—

| | |
|---|---|
| 1939 | Born in Naju, Jeollanam-do. |
| 1959 | Became an apprentice at a tailor shop. |
| 1984 | Started a tailor shop of his own as part of Kookmin Bank's Consumers Cooperative. |
| 1994 | Became chair of the Seoul Apparel Labor Union. |
| 1997 | Included in the 2,000 "Progressive Leaders" of our society in journal *Mal*. |
| 2009 | Founded the Tailors Academy. |
| 2013 | Partnered up with Delicacy, an Italian tailored suit brand, and started Delicacy Korea. |
| Present | Works as the head of the Tailors Academy. |

The recent phenomenon of looking for and praising decades-old shops and stores among Korean bloggers and Web users began years ago when the mad search for restaurants and diners offering the ultimate taste experience began. Bloggers, in search of genuine and ever diverse food, began to look to restaurants and diners that have been running for generations and came to turn their attention to shops and stores in other businesses as well. If a restaurant or a store that has been running for five decades is valued so much, shouldn't individuals who have practiced the same trade for at least five decades be accorded as much honor and respect as well?

The subject for this chapter in Kim Eui-gon, a tailor who has been making custom-made suits for his clients in a corner of Cheongdam-dong, the most upscale and trendiest district in Seoul, for 57 years on end. There he heads a local institution named the Tailors Academy. Standing right next to Kim's high-end tailor-made suit shop, Peach Line Homme, the Academy offers the prospect of learning and mastering the craft of tailoring.

Peach Line Homme boasts a classical and elegant indoor atmosphere that has been built up and perfected over decades. We may have thought that the demand for tailor-made suits has all but disappeared amid the flood of quality suits mass-produced in factories. A visit to this shop, however, will instantly prove us wrong, with numerous incomplete suits hanging on mannequins and fabric boards here and there. Next to the tailor-made suits is a well-organized selection of fine dress shirts in various colors.

Kim, now in his mid-70s, looked quite good in his own tailor-made suit when I visited him. He has spent more than half a century in tailoring. He was the perfect source from whom I could inquire about the past and future of tailor-made suits in Korea.

# Tailor-Made Suits Were a Crucial Component for a Gentleman, and Tailoring One of the Best Jobs

———

"I hear that large fashion corporations in Korea have decided to forgo their non-compete stance toward tailor-made suit businesses. These corporations are ruthless in their pursuit of profit, and will eventually make people like us vanish from the industry." Kim began the interview with these worries.

Kim wanted to start the interview first and foremost by speaking of the struggles that tailors face in the Korean apparel industry today. About eight years ago, the Korean government placed tailor-made businesses on the list of businesses with which large corporations shall not compete. The list never had the binding force of law, but effectively pressured large corporations to make "concessions" to certain businesses so as not to appear to be greedy. There are no known data showing the exact extent of effectiveness this kind of measure has had, but the list has been shrinking, according less and less protection for craftspeople like Kim. The government needs either to extend or replace the list with other effective measures, but neither the government nor the tailors' association shows any signs of interest in the matter.

In Korea, it has been the norm for large corporations to eat away at smaller businesses' profits and drive them out of the market, with large franchise department stores eradicating local shops, large corporatized bakeries driving out local bakers, and large bookstores expelling small bookshops. The same dog-eat-dog logic applies to the apparel industry as well. But Kim still recalls the day when tailor-made suits were regarded very highly in Korea.

"Back in the 1960s and the 1970s, it was a great honor for Korean men to own and wear tailor-made suits. The best of these suits came from old

Peach Line Homme boasts a classical and elegant indoor atmosphere that has been built up and perfected over decades. We may have thought that the demand for tailor-made suits has all but disappeared amid the flood of quality suits mass-produced in factories. A visit to this shop, however, will instantly prove us wrong, with numerous incomplete suits hanging on mannequins and fabric boards here and there.

neighborhoods in Seoul such as Sogong-dong, Myeongdong and Gwanggyo. According to official records, the first tailor shop in Korea came into being at Sogong-dong, but Gwanggyo grew to become the largest district for tailoring, serving as the center of men's fashion from the 1960s to the early 1980s. Sogong-dong is now more famous because it used to house the Korea Stock Exchange. Money naturally attracted men interested in showing off their power by owning things fine. Sogong-dong was also home to high-fashion boutiques like Andre Kim and numerous flourishing men's suit stores."

**Were those decades the heyday of your career as well?**

Yes, they were. I was in my mid-thirties when it all began. I was a happy man then, making tailor-made suits for some of Korea's most popular celebrities at the time, such as Kim Jin-gyu and Shin Yeong-gyun. People looked up to me as an expert in my field.

**How did you come to enter this world of tailor-made suits in the first place?**

Right after I graduated from high school in 1959, I looked for work in this field. The emphasis of the high school curriculum at the time was that every graduate should have at least one trade with which he or she could earn his or her living. My father worked all his life as a civil servant, and never knew to enrich himself or his family by taking bribes and gifts. My family was poor even by the standard of those days. It was my father who suggested that I should earn more income by learning a trade. Tailoring was considered one of the most lucrative and promising professions at the time, so I chose this field.

**Where did you start to learn?**

I was lucky to meet a great teacher from my first try. My uncle — the husband of my father's sister — took me in as his apprentice and gave me years of intensive and practical lessons. In just a year and a half of starting out in this field, I was able to make a blazer all on my own. Back then, it was common for young apprentices in my field to idle away for years at the beginning of their career, running errands and not learning much about their trade. Fortunately for me, I did not have to waste my time like that, and was able to learn my craft quickly.

**How was the working environment at tailor shops in the 1960s?**

Young apprentices had to do a lot of things before a shop opened for the day, the most important of which was to have the iron flamed and warmed. Back then, we had no electric irons. We all had to work by warming up our irons in charcoal fires. All tailor shops had charcoal pits in their backyards. Young apprentices would sleep behind piles of charcoal, not afraid to get their clothes and bodies dirty, because they were always so tired.

**Do you remember the first blazer you made?**

Of course I do! I was so proud of my work and it seemed flawlessly beautiful to me. Back then, craftspeople like my uncle worked mostly as subcontractors. My uncle was so respected and skilled that he was able to call a price 30 percent higher than his fellow tradesmen. But I knew not a thing about tailoring, so the first blazer I made looked as good to me as any of the suits my uncle made.

**I am sure your uncle would have begged to differ.**

Yes, he would have. It was only years later that I finally came to see the huge difference between my first work and his creations.

**You just mentioned that your uncle was able to charge a higher fee or price because he was skilled. Are things the same for tailors today?**

Yes, they are. It is natural that the market pays higher prices for products from better producers. Master craftspeople should be treated according to their expertise and experience, shouldn't they?

**They must have been, especially during the heyday of tailor-made suits in Korea.**

"I was in my mid-thirties when it all began. I was a happy man then, making tailored suits for some of Korea's most popular celebrities at the time, such as Kim Jin-gyu and Shin Yeong-gyun. Peopled looked up to me as an expert in my field."

In the 1970s, the largest and most popular suit business in Korea was Mirim Tailor Shop. The business generated larger annual revenue than a large construction company at the time. Stylish gentlemen walked down the street of Myeongdong in their three-piece tailor-made suits, and tailors were held in high regard. Almost all tailor shops boasted awards they had won at international competitions.

# People Will Return to Tailor-Made Suits One Day

———

Kim appeared thrilled to talk about how Korean tailors were widely respected and admired around the world.

"Back then, there was a public tailoring competition in Korea, focusing solely on blazers and not trousers. Koreans are really good at making things with their hands. The first International Vocational Training Competition started in the early 1960s. Korean tailors topped the competition for 12 years in a row, from 1967 to 1983. We even made our way into the *Guinness Book of World Records*, which remains unbroken. The tailoring category was ultimately removed from the competition because there was no way for participants from other countries to beat the Koreans."

**Why do you think the Koreans so excelled?**

Participants from advanced countries were rookies who had barely entered their fields, while Korean contestants were professionals with years of experience. This is because most Korean tailors started learning their trade immediately after graduating from elementary school, and learned and mastered their craft so quickly that they became skilled craftspeople capable of charging higher fees or prices by the age of 20. It was natural for these extremely experienced young people to win the gold medal at every competition. Our counterparts from other countries, on the other hand, started learning their trade after high school. They were simply not experienced enough by the time they entered these competitions with us.

**But the tailoring industry began to decline in the 1970s, didn't it?**

Until the 1970s, "suits" equaled tailor-made suits, and Korean tailors also received a lot of orders from Japan. As factories began to produce large quantities of machine-made suits, however, people were no longer willing to pay the higher prices for tailor-made suits. With the steady drop in demand, we have been unable to teach and train a new generation of tailors over the last two decades.

**Are there any hopes for the tailor-made suit business?**

Yes, there are. I see that the demand for our products has begun to revive. Suit fabric dealers are the most perceptive observers of this market, and they tell me that Korea still has at least several companies specializing in producing fabrics for suits. There is no such company in Japan now. However, I see that the suit market in Korea is increasingly polarized, with the middle disappearing rapidly. There are dozens of stores dealing in very luxurious Italian-made suits in Korea. There are also a growing number of consumers not willing to pay more than KRW 500,000 per suit. There are fewer consumers in between these segments. Nevertheless, more and more Korean consumers seek to express their individuality through rare brand-name items and custom-made things. We Koreans are especially fashion-sensitive. I am optimistic that the demand for tailor-made suits will grow in the future.

**You believe that people will eventually come around and value tailor-made suits again.**

The goal of clothing manufacturers is to produce clothes that are just like tailor-made ones. Tailor-made suits are intended to serve their wearers only and no one else. They are customized to the physical characteristics and needs of their wearers. Factory-manufactured clothes, on the other hand, can be worn by anyone in the ballpark range of standard sizes. They fail to fit as well or be as comfortable for the wearer as tailor-made suits do. Fashion is increasingly becoming an instrument of identity and expression, so people will eventually return to tailor-made suits.

**What efforts do you think tailors need to make to see a revival of their trade?**

Marketing is the most important effort they should make. Tailor-made shops cannot remain long in business only with returning customers. We tailors need to cultivate our business strategies as much as our skills, but we are less interested in those matters. I, myself, have focused almost all my time on making suits and not anything else. We Koreans won the international competition for 12 years in a row. This country is flooded with gifted tailors. Few of them, however, ever made it to genuine success. They all possessed great skill, but paid little attention to design or pattern-making and had almost no interest in marketing. The winners of the international competition would have thrived, had they had support and training on customer management and marketing. These award-winning tailors and their businesses eventually vanished as they came to lose the few returning customers they had.

"The goal of clothing manufacturers is to produce clothes that
are just like tailor-made ones. Tailor-made suits are intended
to serve their wearers only and no one else. They are customized
to the physical characteristics and needs of their wearers."

# The Master Tailor Makes All His Suits Comfortable for Their Wearers

——

Kim believes that the skill to make a perfect blazer or pair of trousers is great and useful, but also thinks that tailors should not expect to survive and thrive on self-satisfaction alone. One may be able to create the world's most perfect and comfortable suit, but still needs communication skills with clients.

Peach Line Homme provides a good example. The shop, with six employees now, is located in Cheongdam-dong, into which the latest and most luxurious fashion flows. Kim explained his decision to locate his business there. "That is because I thought Cheongdam-dong could very well become the next Sogong-dong. We not only tailor-make new suits for our clients, but also re-do the upscale suits that clients already own. Consumers of high-end suits in Korea today pay for the brand more than the quality of the suits they purchase. Well-known brand-name fashion houses abide by standard sizes based on golden ratios. Tailoring is about breaking away from those golden ratios to suit particular wearers' needs. A well-made European suit cannot make a typical Korean consumer comfortable because, for instance, of the difference in the length of the arms. Europeans have longer arms than Koreans. So it is my job as a tailor to repair and modify such suits according to my clients' orders. Repairing requires as much skill as does tailoring. That is why they come to us."

**Are there any specific characteristics or criteria that a suit must meet?**

That it should not stand out. Suits used to be the attire of Western men, but they have become universal business attire for men of all races and ethnicities worldwide now. In other words, suits must be comfortable to the wearer. The master tailor is someone who makes all his suits comfortable for their wearers.

The secret to a comfortable suit is in pattern-making. Italian suits dominate the world because they are light and comfortable to wear.

**Tailoring is a handicraft that requires highly advanced skills, but I have not seen many schools offering formal lessons.**

Fashion and apparel departments at Korean colleges and universities produce over 8,000 graduates each year, but none of these departments ever teach anything in-depth about men's suits. Women's clothing may appear to require greater skill and delicacy, but the truth is that men's suits are among the most difficult to make. This is because 80 to 90 percent of the entire suit making process requires the use of real human hands. In order for one to make a perfect suit for a man, one must pay thorough attention to all the invisible details. That is why well-tailored suits do not change shape even after decades.

**Students who come to your Tailors Academy must have made up their minds to dedicate their lives to tailoring.**

That is true. Many of my students are people with college degrees in fashion- or apparel-related subjects. I founded this Academy at my late an age because I believe in the importance of educating and training skilled tailors. Tailor-made suits are no longer a focus of consumer attention not only because of dwindling demand, but also because of the fewer skilled tailors. I was able to start the Academy in 2010 with the support from the Korean government's Labor-Management Relations Committee program, but the government support stopped coming in as of 2014.

**How many graduates has the Tailors Academy produced?**

We have had about 260 graduates so far, who work not only in men's suits, but across all fields of fashion. The Academy currently trains about 20 students, who are all hired as apprentices at actual tailor shops. My hope is to see more and more talented tailors who are skilled not only at making good suits, but

*"Suits must be comfortable for the wearer.
The master tailor is someone who makes all his suits
comfortable for their wearers."*

also at marketing.

**How long does it take one to become a full tailor?**

It takes about two years of learning and training to be able to create a decent blazer on one's own. To make a really good blazer and charge a higher fee, though, you need at least five years. Koreans are used to fast change and fast growth, and often neglect the role of time and effort in the process. I always stress the rule of 10,000 hours to my students.

**You mean the rule that one has to invest at least three hours a day for 10 years to succeed in one's field?**

That's right. Of course, the number "10,000" is more of a guideline than a rule. A real expert knows when he or she has reached a certain level of mastery over his or her craft. My uncle spent most of his life tailoring suits, but quit one day without hesitation. Companies tried to recruit him out of his retirement, but he would not budge. He explained that he retired because he could no longer create what he used to create. That is when I realized what a true master really looks like in old age. I respected his lifetime work and his uncompromising standard, so stopped trying to persuade him to go back to work.

Kim told me that, until the 1970s or so, tailors used to complain of the stress they got while trying to make really good suits. By the 1980s, few tailors ever complained of the difficulty of making satisfactory suits because all they cared about was money.

# Being a Spokesperson for Tailors

Fifty-seven years have elapsed since Kim first began learning about tailoring at age 20. Kim is 77 years old now, well past the age of retirement even by his industry's standard. He appreciates the fact that age is an asset and not a liability in the field of tailoring. He has been contributing to tailoring not only with the quality of the suits he has made, but also through his advocacy work. He started his labor activism in 1971, and chaired the Seoul Apparel Labor Union (SALU) from 1994 to 2010. He still remains on the board of the union as a senior advisor. The union, affiliated with the Federation of Korean Textile Distribution Workers' Unions, currently has about 170 members. There are over 1,000 tailors and tailor-made suit distributors across Korea.

"SALU was established in 1948 as an association of tailors, a profession regarded as white-collar and well-paid while Korea was under Japanese colonial rule. The first several chairmen of the union were all labor activists. I have heard from my predecessors that tailors were at first encouraged to join labor union and movements, but were subjected to increasing persecution later as they began to place increasing demands on their employers."

**I am impressed that tailors began unionizing so early.**

We have been active in the labor movements in Korea. During the last years of the Liberal Party, we even went on major strikes in opposition to society-wide corruption and unfairness. We combined forces in objection to the excessive business practices of Jangmi, a tailor shop owned by Cheil Woolen Fabrics. We also launched a boycott campaign against Cheil in the mid-1980s when the company released Galaxy, the brand for Korea's first factory-produced men's suits. SALU was re-launched as an affiliate of the Federation of Korean Textile

Distribution Workers' Union in 1988.

**That was a year after the major workers' strife of 1987, wasn't it?**

Yes, it was that strife that inspired us to re-organize the union and hold our inauguration ceremony in August 1988. The ceremony gathered about 2,000 tailors from across Seoul at the time. Our collective-bargaining practices have done much to raise the wages for tailors and give them paid vacations.

**What do you think will take for the tailoring industry today to take the next great leap forward?**

I have been saying repeatedly that Korean tailors are already the world's best in terms of skills. They lag behind their Italian counterparts, though, because of their lack of marketing efforts. With adequate marketing support, though, Korean tailors can thrive on the world market with their attention to detail and their great skill. Many Korean tailors emigrated to South America in the 1960s as quality assurance inspectors because their ability to discern good suits from bad was greatly valued at the time. It is not that Koreans lack the capability to create world-class suits. But Korean consumers themselves prefer expensive foreign brands over Korean-made suits. Like other industries, tailoring can globalize successfully when it already has a thriving domestic market.

**I hear that you have been making new attempts through Peach Line Homme.**

We have teamed up with Delicacy, an Italian brand for tailor-made suits. The company has produced suits for such world figures as Barack Obama, Bill Clinton and John Kerry. Now we have launched the brand of Delicacy Korea here. We present ready-made clothes to upscale customers at high-end department stores, and use those clothes to attract them to tailor-made suits as well.

**Would you recommend to today's young Koreans that they should adopt tailoring as a lifetime career?**

*"It is not that Koreans lack the capability to create world-class suits.
But Korean consumers themselves prefer expensive foreign brands over
Korean-made suits."*

At the Tailors Academy, young men, all dressed quite comfortably but also stylishly, were working intently on making the suits assigned them. They were all working on something different, but seemed to be united by their focus on becoming the best tailors they could be.

Clothes are our second skin. Every man wants to own at least one really good suit. I have no doubt that the demand for tailoring will begin to grow in the coming years, and this field needs a lot of young and talented people to meet that demand. Tailoring has long been neglected as a declining trade, so its doors are wide open and competition still very low. Young people have much to hope for in this field.

After our interview ended, Kim volunteered to show me around the Tailors Academy. When I stepped into it right next door to his tailor shop, I could not help but admire what I saw. The Academy reminded me of the workspace of some high-end Italian brand, with its young men, all dressed quite comfortably but also stylishly, working intently on making the suits assigned them.

One man was stitching a pair of trousers using a sewing machine; another, hand-stitching a piece of round-shaped fabric; and another, about to cut out a given piece of fabric. They were all working on something different, but seemed to be united by their focus on becoming the best tailors they could be. I had a chance to talk to a young man named Lee Jong-seok, for whom it had been barely a month since he was honorably discharged from the military. When I asked him why he chose to learn about tailoring, he answered: "I want to become really good at this job. There is a difference between distribution and production. In production, I can be proud of what I create. Of course, production can also be challenging and difficult. I do not care whether or not I make a lot of money. But I want to live a life doing something that makes me proud."

As Kim listened to his student, he could not hide a broad smile that appeared on his face. Why Kim could continue to pursue a single path for his entire life was evident in the answer given by his young pupil.

# Kim
# Jong-mok

—

Master Jewelry Maker
43 years of work

## Reclaiming Korea's Position as a
## Leading Global Center for Jewelry Production

—

| | |
|---|---|
| 1957 | Born in Yangyang, Gangwon-do. |
| 1973 | Moved to Seoul and entered a program on jewelry making and appraisal. |
| 1981 | Won the bronze medal at the International Vocational Training Competition in Atlanta. |
| 1981 | Opened his own business, Lucky Jewelry, on Chungmu-ro, Seoul. |
| 1990 | Won the gold medal at the Korea National Master-Level Vocational Training Competition, and became a government-recognized "master" craftsman. |
| 1997 | Founded MJC Vocational Training College for jewelry making. |
| Present | CEO of MK Jewelry Incorporated and Kim Jong-mok Jewelry; President of the Korea Jeweler Confederation Associate; Chairman of the Seoul Jewelry Promotion Foundation. |

The undisputed capital of Korea's jewelry industry is Jongno 3-ga in Seoul. There are over 3,000 jewelry shops and distributors located on this street. Many Koreans travel there to celebrate special occasions in their lives, such as their weddings, the first birthdays of their children, and anniversaries, for gold, silver and gemstones are universally popular for marking and celebrating special moments in life.

At 10 a.m., the jewelry street was slowly awakening to the start of another new day as I made my visit to MJC Vocational Training College. Lotte Cinema, a large corporate multiplex, has replaced the once-famous Piccadilly Theater. It was at the school, situated on the eighth floor of the multiplex building, that I met Kim Jong-mok, the founder of the school and the master jewelry maker who is the subject of this chapter.

Numerous lecture rooms on both sides of the hallway already had dozens of students listening intently to lecturers. The founding chairman's office was humble and undecorated, and the atmosphere about the entire school was calm and tranquil. Kim's greeting message in the school prospectus reads as follows: "You will bear the fruit of a miracle if you choose a career path wisely in accordance with your aptitude and passion, and continue pursuing it with determination and perseverance." They were not just empty words. A renowned jewelry maker in Korea, Kim was telling prospective students what he realized from his own life experience.

Kim told me that he immediately set out to establish this school when he knew he had achieved major success in his field. He did so because he knew how important it is to educate and train subsequent generations of jewelers in order to ensure the future of the industry.

# A Profession Once Treated as Criminal

——

I asked him how he had embarked upon this path of master jeweler over four decades ago. Born and raised in the small provincial town of Yangyang in Gangwon-do, Kim made his way to Seoul at a young age in the 1970s.

"After I moved here, I kept wondering what I could do for living. There were major subway construction works going on everywhere in downtown Seoul at the time, so I considered briefly working as a heavy equipment technician. I also entertained the idea of becoming a quality assurance inspector. While looking about here and there for possible work, I happened upon a small private school offering lessons on jewelry making and appraisal. After a meeting with the school counselor, I immediately enrolled myself. I had been good at making things with my hands as a child and the whole idea seemed interesting to me."

**Back in your day, it must have been unheard of for people to enroll in schools in order to learn a trade. Didn't most people then think that a trade was something one could learn only while training and working in the field rather than by taking lessons at a formal school?**

They did indeed. It still amazes me how I got the idea of enrolling myself in that program so quickly. The program cost KRW 20,000 a month, when the typical wage for field laborers at the time was KRW 2,000 a month. It cost me a fortune — KRW 120,000 — to take and complete that six-month program. It was an amount of money a worker could imagine making only by saving all his wages for six years without spending a penny. There were only one or two such schools offering jewelry making lessons in Seoul at the time. All the students enrolled at these schools were grownups much older than me. These grownups wanted to learn jewelry making in search of better careers or trying to emigrate

*Numerous lecture rooms on both sides of the hallway already had dozens of students listening intently to lecturers.*

overseas.

**Was the program worth your money and time?**

The theoretical knowledge I developed at the school did give me a firm foundation on which I could continue with my practice. It certainly enhanced my ability to apply and adapt various designs and techniques. A school diploma wasn't considered anything of value in my field at the time. All jewelry makers, whether educated or not, started out as apprentices. The only advantage I had at the time was that I could practice my techniques alone at the school in the evening. These practice hours, though, helped me improve my skills much more rapidly.

**How were working conditions at jewelry workshops at the time?**

We all dealt with these sparkling and beautiful objects, but our workshops were poorly lit and often lacked any connection to waterworks. We technicians would spend hours working in dust and with grit. We needed water to wash our hands, so we would go to the building next door and steal some tap water in secret. Jewelry-making was an illegal trade at the time. All jewelry in Korea had been smuggled from sources overseas. We would turn off all the lights in our workshops and lie on the ground, holding our breath, whenever we heard that some customs agents were coming our way. Those agents would order us to lift our hands from whatever we were working on and take away all the gemstones and gold powder from our work tables.

**You paid all that money to learn jewelry making. Didn't it bother you to have paid such a high price for working in a trade where you were treated as a criminal?**

It bothered me greatly. I started out in this career with a great ambition, but almost came to quit after a week or so of starting out. I seriously thought about returning to my hometown and becoming a father like the adults in my family.

"We all dealt with these sparkling and beautiful objects, but our workshops were poorly lit and often lacked any connection to waterworks. Not only that, but jewelry making was also an illegal trade at the time. All jewelry in Korea had been smuggled from sources overseas."

My friends and colleagues, though, kept telling me to be patient for at least a month.

**And the one month became four decades of the single-hearted pursuit of your craft.**

I practiced and worked at my technique day in and day out. Over time, I came not to mind anything else at all. That is how jewelry making became my lifetime career. I ran countless errands and polished countless stones. But I took delight in all these menial tasks. I was especially excited to draw my designs on pieces of paper and then realize them using real jewelry.

**Tell me more about the first workshop you worked at.**

It was a sizable workshop that mainly focused on designing and polishing jewelry. The workshop employed almost 20 people.

**Did you stand out from the 20 employees with your gift?**

I am not sure if I was born with a gift for this career. But I am sure I was among the hardest-working. I was the one who would show up at work the earliest and leave work the latest, whether during the week or on the weekends. The owner of the workshop used to be the one who showed up for work the earliest and left the latest before I came along. Three months later, the owner handed me the keys to the workshop so that I could unlock and lock the door. I was grateful for being recognized like that and worked even harder afterward.

# A Master Jeweler and a Mentor to the Future Generation of Korean Jewelers

---

It was natural for a hardworking and gifted jeweler like Kim to compete in a major international competition and show off his skills to the world.

"Four years after starting work in jewelry, in 1981, I traveled to Atlanta to attend the International Vocational Training Competition. The Korean delegation beat the Japanese and won the Grand Prize for the fourth year in a row. We returned to Korea to wide acclaim and praise, having beat the Japanese against whom Koreans still held much resentment at the time."

**You must remember that victory very well even now.**

We rode along a car parade between Gimpo Airport and Gwanghwamun all day long. The delegation had 31 contestants in total, and we were all treated and welcomed like national heroes! There were countless interviews and congratulatory banquets awaiting us. We were so busy with these events that the disbanding ceremony could not be held for a whole month.

**Things must have worked out very well for you afterward.**

I was lucky enough to open my own business, Lucky Jewelry, on Chungmu-ro in Seoul shortly after I returned from the competition. It was the heyday of the jewelry industry in Korea. Diamond dealers were concentrated in and around Lotte Department Store in Myeongdong at the time. The name "Kim Jong-mok" came to carry significant weight in that diamond district as something of a guarantee for hard work and quality. Orders started flooding my business. I had to work until very late almost every night to meet all those orders.

**You had achieved major success already by your mid-30s. Didn't you also become a government-recognized "master" craftsman in 1990?**

*"I am among the first such master craftsman to be recognized. There are over 500 such master craftspeople alive in Korea today. I was the 25th to be named thus and the third in the field of jewelry."*

Yes, I am among the first such master craftsman to be recognized. There are over 500 such master craftspeople alive in Korea today. I was the 25th to be named thus and the third in the field of jewelry. The criteria for assessing candidates for the title of "master" were much more rigorous than those applied today. We had to win regional and national contests.

**What does it mean to you to bear that honor?**

I had always been apologetic for the fact that I won only a bronze medal at the international competition in 1981, when others and I had expected a gold medal. The experience taught me something invaluable, though. If I won a gold medal so easily at that competition, I would have become so arrogant and rude that I would never have bothered to learn more afterward. I had been the best in my field in Korea for years, so I needed that experience to realize that there were and will always be people who are better than me.

In 1997, Kim founded Maestro Jewelry College, now known as MJC Vocational Training College, convinced that formal education and training were indispensable to the development of the next generation of expert jewelers, and, consequently, to the growth of the Korean jewelry industry. He spent all his time, passion and wealth on creating the best possible jewelry school in Korea. The process of obtaining authorization from the Ministry of Labor for the school was quite laborious and cumbersome. After much trial and error, MJC Vocational Training College has finally been accredited by the Ministry of Education, authorized to grant college diplomas and bachelor's degrees. The school currently trains 200 to 300 students, having produced over 5,000 graduates so far.

MJC Vocational Training College is the only institution in the world that specializes solely in the education and training of jewelry making and appraisal.

Kim is confident that it also offers the best faculty and facilities on jewelry in Korea. The school is gaining fame overseas, so much so that a French student has recently completed his training at the school and gotten his diploma. The school has also entered a memorandum of understanding with Beijing University and has plans to open a satellite school in Nigeria. Kim could not hide the look of pride from his face when he talked about his students who went on to win the gold medals at international competitions. (Lee Geun-gyu and Kang Ga-ram, both graduates of MJC, won the gold medals at the International Vocational Training Competitions in India and Japan in 2004 and 2007, respectively.)

# Infinite Potential and Prospects for the Korean Jewelry Industry
—

Kim still runs his own jewelry business aside from working at the school. MK Jewelry, located at the heart of Gangnam — that most expensive of all land in Korea — deals in world-class jewelry. Since early in 2014, Kim has also been actively working as the President of the Korea Jeweler Confederation Associate, trying to imbue the industry with new energy and inspiration. He now represents a major nationwide federation that encompasses 18 trade associations across all subfields of the jewelry industry.

Since he took the position, Kim has refused to follow in the footsteps of his predecessors. Rather than having his inauguration ceremony in a hotel, as his predecessors did, Kim insisted on having it at his school. The first job he did in his official capacity was to take, voluntarily, the program on tax affairs at the National Tax Service. He then organized a public hearing on legitimizing the jewelry trade in Korea and visited the Tax System Office at the Ministry of Strategy and Finance to make a public promise that jewelers would make effort to pay all their taxes. He then set out on a personal campaign, encouraging fellow jewelers to be honest taxpayers. This series of activities has perplexed many in the industry, but Kim explains that all these activities were necessary, for he believes that jewelers cannot afford to stay complacent and persist in old habits and practices if they truly care about the future of their trade.

"The biggest problem facing the jewelry industry today is that the government authorities refuse to recognize the great potential this industry has for creating jobs and adding high value. The Korean jewelry market is valued at KRW 5.1 trillion, among the 10 largest jewelry markets around the world. The industry already employs well over 200,000 people. We Korean jewelers are also praised worldwide for our skills."

**I have done some research, and found that Korean jewelers won the gold medal at the International Vocational Training Competition four times between 2007 and 2013 and the Grand Prize 18 times. There is no doubt that Koreans are among the most skilled in the world, so why does Korean jewelry lack as much commercial appeal?**

Korean-made fashion accessories are already the world's best in terms of quality. We may not have well-known brand names, but it does not mean that we lack skilled jewelry makers. Fashion accessories are mostly made of metals and therefore affordable to make. That is why we have rapidly become the world's leader in this regard. The Chinese may be quickly catching up with us, but the world knows that Korean jewelry far surpasses its Chinese counterpart in terms of quality and added value. If we switched from cheap metals to gemstones, why shouldn't we be able to establish well-known brand names?

**Are you saying that Koreans are the best at making fashion accessories, but not jewelry?**

The Korean jewelry industry is declining rather than growing. Individual jewelers in Korea have striven for decades, investing their personal wealth and time into developing the industry so that Korean jewelers are now among the most skilled in the world. One cannot imagine how much more growth we would have achieved by now with systematic government support. I am not demanding that the government give us more money. All I am asking is that the government loosen its tight regulatory hand on us. The excise tax on items of jewelry is the biggest obstacle to the industry's growth now. It must be abolished at all costs. With such regulatory hindrance gone, the Korean jewelry industry will begin to grow dramatically.

**What do you think is the solution to the current problem?**

The only way out of the decline is to make jewelers go legitimate. And the only way to achieve that is if the government abolished the excise tax on jewelry. Large corporations made headways into the jewelry market in the past, but they had to shut down not long afterward because the heavy taxes levied made competitive pricing impossible. Even foreign investors attempted to do business in Korea, but all have ultimately left.

**The Korean government has been categorizing jewelry as a "luxury good" since 1976, imposing excise taxes on it alongside liquor, golf courses, casinos and petroleum. Are you saying this tax policy is hindering the growth of the jewelry industry today?**

That is precisely what I mean. Say you came to my shop as a customer. If I told you that you could purchase the item of your choice either at the full price, 36 percent of which is taxes (10-percent value-added tax and 26-percent excise tax) or at a reduced price by paying with cash, wouldn't you feel tempted to do the latter? That is why illegal jewelry transactions off the books continue to thrive in Korea, as a result of which the government itself cannot collect as much value-added and excise taxes as it aims to. Jewelry is something that the government cannot control. Just as in the case of items of apparel or other general merchandise, people should be able to purchase jewelry by paying only the minimum tax. How can the jewelry market grow and contribute to the national economy with such heavy tax burdens?

**The excise tax does not seem to function as planned, does it?**

A recent Gallup survey estimated the total worth of the Korean jewelry market to amount to KRW 5.2 trillion. We industry insiders, on the other hand, think that it amounts to at least KRW 10 trillion. The government, in theory, should be able to collect KRW 500 billion in value-added taxes alone from an industry that is worth KRW 5 trillion, but the government has collected KRW 120 billion only so far. The National Tax Service has collected a meager KRW 5 billion only from jewelry in excise taxes because the vast majority of jewelry transactions take place off the books, with more and more consumers making their purchases abroad. The government is not doing a good job in either tax collecting or preventing smuggling.

**The excise tax appears to have encouraged jewelers and buyers to go under the table.**

That is right. That is why I keep telling people that it is best to deregulate the jewelry industry so that we jewelers would be willing to pay our taxes voluntarily, creating more jobs and doing much more for the national economy. Korean consumers pay value-added taxes even on the little snacks that their children enjoy, so why should the Korean government be unable to collect fair and due taxes from much pricier jewelry?

**But you know that many still believe that such high excise taxes on luxury**

*"The biggest problem facing the jewelry industry today is that the government authorities refuse to recognize the great potential this industry has for creating jobs and adding high value."*

**goods like jewelry are fair and rational.**

People like to complain that the wealthy are not taxed enough, either on the income they earn or on the purchases of high-end items they make. Such complaints sound rational only on the surface though. We may keep high taxes insofar as the government can really collect them and put them to good use. However, the current tax system fails to work and instead only serves to encourage illegal transactions. That is why we have to reform it.

**What are other added benefits of abolishing the excise tax on jewelry?**

It will help the jewelry industry create more jobs. The industry hires over 200,000 people, but the official statistics report only 30,000. That is because jewelers have increased their businesses through illegal transactions and are afraid to report increases in the number of their employees, for fear of having to disclose their books. Abolish the excise tax and encourage jewelers to go legitimate, and the government will instantly be able to see an increase of at least 60,000 registered employees, which will also significantly lower the unemployment rate.

**Is there enough room for more jobs in the jewelry industry?**

There are about 80 colleges and universities in Korea that offer jewelry-related programs. The number would increase to over 100 if we counted vocational training and private (unaccredited) schools as well. Almost 3,000 people graduate from these programs each year. Why do these programs persist? Because people know that, by taking these programs, they can land jobs. The jewelry industry does exist and thrive, but all under the table.

# Korea Has Lost Its Business to Thailand and Hong Kong

—

Kim's central message to the public is that the Korean jewelry industry can flourish and contribute meaningfully to the national economy only when the excise tax is abolished.

"Of the member states of the Organization for Economic Cooperation and Development (OECD), China and Korea are the only countries that levy excise taxes on jewelry. The current tax regime also prevents overseas manufacturers and buyers from doing more business with Korean jewelers."

**I hear that the jewelry industries in other Asian countries, such as Thailand, are growing rapidly in contrast to Korea's.**

While we Korean jewelers have been trapped in the excise tax dilemma, our neighboring countries have taken away our customers and business. The jewelry industry in Thailand was still in an incipient stage in 1983, but has grown at an astonishing speed ever since, and is now one of the three largest industries in the country. The Thai jewelry industry hires over two million people, with well-known European jewelry brands setting their jewelry in Thailand. That is something we Koreans should have done a long time ago. We are much better skilled than our Thai counterparts. You don't even see Thai contestants at international competitions. Yet, whenever a new Prime Minister wins an election in Thailand, he or she first goes to see the president of the Thai jewelry association.

**Isn't Hong Kong also a major competitor?**

The jewelry industry in Hong Kong took root in the mid-1990s, but is not among the 10 largest industries in the city-state. Hong Kong organizes four major jewelry fairs a year, which are among the most influential and biggest of their kind in the world. These fairs attract participants from over 50 countries around the world, earning over KRW 400 billion from booth rental alone. Korean businesses also attend these fairs, although to do so costs each business at least KRW 100 million. Why is this waste necessary? Given our skills and craft, we could have launched similar or even more successful events a long time ago, attracting international clients to our side instead of spending our own money to visit fairs overseas.

**The jewelry industry began in Korea four decades ago, but it has stopped growing under government neglect.**

That is so. In terms of skills and quality alone, we have no reason to lag so far behind the jewelry industries of other countries. The Chinese still have to wait a long time before they finally catch up with us. We have expert craftspeople, excellent designers and hardworking employees. Many of our jewelry craftspeople have emigrated overseas to work under better conditions. They may remit some of their money back to Korea, but our cost in terms of brain drain is much greater. At any rate, you can rest assured that Korean jewelers are the world's most skilled.

**Why don't we consider jewelry as part of fashion so as to enhance the added value of jewelry?**

I believe that is ultimately the way this industry should go in the future. Consumers are well aware of the huge difference jewelry makes to their overall style and fashion. Apparel and jewelry go hand in hand, along with shoes, bags and other such accessories. At any rate, I believe that Korean manufacturers should now begin to compete by producing high-end and high-value-added goods. They can attract foreign investors and consumers only by convincing them of the great value they could have by purchasing goods made in Korea.

"In terms of skills and quality alone, we have no reason to lag so far behind the jewelry industries of other countries. The Chinese still have to wait a long time before they finally catch up with us. We have expert craftspeople, excellent designers and hardworking employees."

Kim continues to emphasize that the jewelry industry holds the key to the future of the Korean creative economy. He is convinced that encouraging jewelry transactions to go legitimate by alleviating the tax burden is the only way to enhance the international competitiveness of Korean jewelry. Even with astonishing advancement in technology, jewelry still requires much manual work from people. As this industry begins to grow, it will naturally come to create more and more jobs. Kim asks what could be a better welfare policy for the future of Korea than providing people with more and better-paying jobs.

When I asked him whether jewelry making is a craft worthy of passing down to the generations, Kim answered by saying that his own son was also learning and training in jewelry craft. He stressed the importance of educating and training younger generations of jewelry makers in order to secure the future of the industry. Jewelers in Korea have long worked on the borderline of the law and failed to cultivate a legitimate sense of pride in their trade. Kim, however, wants to be a proud father and mentor to his son. The master jeweler's old face continued to beam with his passion and devotion to the future of the Korean jewelry industry.

# Ji
# Su-hee

—

Master Dressmaker of Natural Materials
39 years of work

# Wholehearted
# Dressmaking

—

| | |
|---|---|
| 1963 | Born in Hampyeong, Jeollanam-do. |
| 1967 | Moved to Seoul with parents, at age 5. |
| 1976 | Began to work as a dressmaker's *shida* at the Jungbu Market after graduating from elementary school. |
| 1977 | Began to work at a factory producing children's clothes at the Donghwa Market. |
| 1979 | Became a second-in-command sewing machine operator, at age 17 |
| 1981 | Continued to participate in underground labor and democratization activities, while working as a full-time dressmaker, after the Cheonggye Apparel Labor Union was forced to dissolve. |
| 1990 | Continued to make a wide range of clothes, including women's apparel and sportswear, after getting married. |
| 2005 | Began to make clothes of natural materials at a natural-dyed apparel shop at Insa-dong, Seoul. |
| 2007 | Became a member of the Cham Shinnaneun Ot ("Exciting Clothes"), a social enterprise. |
| 2008 | Began to teach natural-material dressmaking at the Korea Academy of Fashion and Sewing. |
| 2009-Present | Runs a workshop of traditional-style and natural-dyed apparel named Yeomim and continues to teach students. |

Some time in August, on one of the last remaining hot days of that summer, I took a subway ride to visit the interviewee for this chapter. I was excited as if I were going to meet an old friend rather than to have a formal interview. The interviewee was someone I became friends with while working in the Cheonggye Apparel Labor Union in the 1980s. I invited her to become a member of Cham Shinnaneun Ot ("Exciting Clothes"), a social enterprise, and also of the Korea Academy of Fashion and Sewing, both of which I began to run, about two decades after our work on the union. The interviewee was now a renowned dressmaker, specializing in natural dyes and materials, of her own right. I was proud of having such a friend.

As I climbed up the staircase of a five-story building in which my interviewee worked, I could tell that the building housed numerous clothes-making workshops and factories. There were huge plastic bags filled with scrap pieces of fabrics at every corner. The interviewee's shop was located on the third floor. It was a plain space, containing only the bare minimum of things that she needed to work. Behind the partition were a sewing machine and an ironing stand attached to each other at one end. In the front of the back wall of the room was a small cabinet containing threads of all colors. On the right side of the cabinet were a series of works awaiting final touches before being transferred to the shop. Ji Su-hee, my friend and the interviewee, emerged from behind the sewing machine with her signature reassuring smile.

"Natural dyeing itself requires much more work and effort than factory dyeing. Factory-style sewing can do harm to these natural-dye fabrics and ultimately undermines their value. That is why these fabrics require a special set of sewing skills and techniques."

# A Conscientious Dressmaker Does Everything for Her Client That Can Be Done by Sewing

———

Natural-dyed fabrics often remind us Koreans of the "reformed" *hanbok* (traditional-style Korean garments) of a modernized style that only the middle-aged and the elderly would wear. Ji's products, however, are so chic in style and design that they can instantly wake out of your stereotype. I have been wearing clothes made by her for decades. On our interview day, I was also wearing a hemp blazer that Ji had made for me. It was my favorite piece of clothing to wear on a scorching summer day because it kept me comfortably cool, accommodated all my needs for outdoor activities, and looked stylish even when it was wrinkled.

**What should I exactly call the kind of work you do? You make clothes with natural materials that have been dyed with natural ingredients. Is it natural-fabric dressmaking or natural-dye dressmaking?**

Well, natural dyeing is a process that can be done only on natural materials and fabrics. I am fine with either term. At the Korea Academy of Fashion and Sewing, I teach a class that is named "natural-fabric dressmaking.

**What do clothes made with natural dyes and fabrics differ from run-of-the-mill factory-made ones?**

Because natural dyeing involves repeated washing and boiling of fabrics, natural-dye fabrics are much more durable than other fabrics and rarely shrink even after washing and wear. I also make sure that these fabrics retain the intended pleats every time I touch and work on them so that their shape would remain intact even years or decades later. Consumers also like these clothes because they can re-dye them into different colors.

**I hear that sewing on natural-dye fabrics can be much trickier than sewing on other fabrics.**

Yes, that is true. Natural dyeing itself requires much more work and effort than factory dyeing. Factory-style sewing can do harm to these natural-dye fabrics and ultimately undermines their value. That is why these fabrics require a special set of sewing skills and techniques.

**How does sewing exactly differ?**

Let's turn this dress upside down and see for ourselves. Look at the shape of the seams. They are clearly distinct from the ones you have seen on normal dresses. There is no over-locking involved. I have also had to cut and sewn up each and every single margin to seam. These stitches are extremely tiny and consistent. You cannot expect this quality of sewing from general factory-made clothes. This kind of clothes takes hours and days to complete. The more time I spend on making them, the better their quality becomes.

**How many tasks are involved in making and completing a dress of this kind?**

First, I spread the fabric on both sides. I make pleats with hands in various parts as intended by the design, and iron the fabric with pleats. Then I place the patterns on it and cut it up. Next is a series of related basic tasks, such as making margins to seam, folding and bending. For parts that require slanted pleats, I also have to perform some basting so that the pleats would not disappear later. Afterward, I fix the body shape and attach the things that need to be attached, such as the front and the back as well as the sleeves. Each seam requires at least two or three stitches. Each time I finish a round of sewing, I iron out the dress. I also cut the margins to seam using scissors each time so that the seams would not get too thick.

**It is quite a laborious process!**

After decades of working in this field, this entire process has become part of me. Now I finish all this in about four hours on average. Even so, my clothes are much more time-consuming than factory-made ones.

**Why don't you hire a hand? Why do you insist on doing everything yourself?**

Don't you think I have tried hired hands? People have difficulty warming up to this process, though. The people I hired had backgrounds in clothes factories. They were used to caring more about quantity than quality. Tailoring and dressmaking of the kind I do require wholehearted attention and devotion. The final products show whether or the maker has been focused and dedicated.

**What do you mean by wholehearted dressmaking?**

It means first and foremost that you have to like dressmaking. Without the love of your profession, you cannot be as creative. I try to make as many variations as possible to the same patterns and designs. I think a conscientious dressmaker does everything for her client that can be done by sewing. Making one same-looking thing after another is boring for myself. A client who is willing to pay all that money (between KRW 400,000 and KRW 500,000 for a dress) isn't probably willing to wear something generic, either. That is why, even while working with the same pattern, I make incisions to one end and cut up and stitch together pieces to the other end.

# Making a Profession Part of Oneself

—

Ji apologized and asked me if we could continue our interview after she finished the thing she was working on. I nodded, rather excited to see a master dressmaker at work. She sat in front of her work stand again and worked on tiny seams using her sewing machine. She turned the clothes inside out, got

"Without the love of your profession, you cannot be as creative.
I try to make as many variations as possible to the same patterns
and designs. I think a conscientious dressmaker does everything
for her client that can be done by sewing."

hold of the seams more tightly, and began to iron them. She repeated this process twice and attached the collar to the blazer. Now a finished hemp blazer was before my eyes. I admired the smoothness and fluency with which she worked.

**I guess sewing is something that involves the work of the human hands no matter how advanced sewing technology is. But I guess natural-fabric dressmaking involves far more work of the hands.**

My hands and sewing machine divide the workload by about five-to-five or six-to-four. Sometimes I imagine what would happen to me if I lost one of my fingers. I use all my ten fingers when I work. Each finger has its own role. These fingers are used to grab the fabric. One exerts a greater force while the other exerts less. This other finger is used to hold the fabric in one place. People tell me that I seem to work effortlessly. That is probably because each and every single one of my fingers does its job perfectly.

**How long did it take you to get to that level of mastery?**

I think it's been five or six years since I felt as if my craft had become part of my body. I feel at one with this work. When I work, I think of nothing else. I keep the radio playing in the background, but I know not a single song it plays. Unless I talk to someone face to face like this, I do not even hear them. I focus entirely on my work because that is what it demands.

**I guess that is the power of immersion. Would you be willing to do the same kind and amount of work on pay for someone else?**

Probably not. I come to work at nine a.m. in the morning and get up to leave at eight p.m. at the earliest. I take no breaks except to have my meals. So I spend quite an amount of time on working every single day. I create three or four clothes at most on a given day. I cannot make all these clothes at once. I have to work and wait for one to finish before I start picking another up. Hanging these clothes side by side at the end of the day, I feel a sense of fulfillment and reward. People ask me whether I do not get tired of repeating all these same tasks all the time. I cannot skip any of them, though, because I know what ruin absent-mindedness can do to this piece of clothes later on. Even though it takes a great period of time, I make sure that I perform every single task that each piece of clothes requires. That is the only way to make sure that these clothes do their job properly.

## An Eyewitness to the Vicissitudes of the Modern Times in Korea
——

**Could you tell me about the life you have led so far?**

I was born in Hampyeong, a small town in the province of Jeollanam-do. My parents were farmers, but had nothing to feed on. So they decided to move to Seoul in search for work. I lived with my grandmother for a while, but eventually moved to Seoul to rejoin my family. I had an older sister and an older brother, and three younger sisters and one younger brother. My older siblings died when they were still teenagers. My older sister used to work as a bus conductor. She was 19 years old when she died, in her small room, of carbon monoxide intoxication from the briquette she burned to heat her room. My older brother was found frozen to death on a street in Noryangjin. I was too young to understand at the time, but people told me later that he had some mental illness. He wasn't born like that, but must have suffered much to adapt to his new life in Seoul. By the time I entered elementary school, at eight years of age, I was the oldest one among my siblings.

"Sometimes I imagine what would happen to me if I lost one of my fingers. I use all my ten fingers when I work. Each finger has its own role."

**That was the tumultuous 1970s, when hundreds of thousands of people kept moving into cities in search of jobs amid Korea's industrialization. What kind of work did your parents do?**

My mother worked as a street vendor. She sold everything she could get her hands on, including fish, fruits and vegetables. My father worked as a janitor at a government building. We lived in one of the hilltop slums in Samyang-dong. At first, we tried to build something resembling a home, using scrap bricks and wooden panels. The veterans that had returned from the Vietnam War at the time began to work as agents of violence on behalf of the government and construction companies, and kept demolishing our humble homes day after day. Later, we decided to pitch a tent for a home. My parents would return from work in the evening and pitch the tent so that we could lie down. By morning we would get up and fold away the tent again. We lived like that for a full decade.

**Like other girls your age, you began working quite early, didn't you?**

Yes, right after I graduated from elementary school, I worked at a bonded clothes factory in Samyang-dong for about three months. After our family moved to Noryangjin, I befriended an older girl, who helped me find a job in dressmaking. I began to work as a *shida* to dressmakers at a factory for making children's clothes at the Jungbu Market, not far from the Pyeonghwa Market. Then I moved to another children's clothes factory at the Donghwa Market and worked there for nine years. I became a sewing machine operator of my own right by the time I was 17 years old.

**Was it around that time that you became acquainted with the Cheonggye Apparel Labor Union?**

That's right. The CALU was known as the Union Shop at the time. It oversaw all the clothes-making shops at the Donghwa Market. At first, I didn't know much about the union, except for the fact that it existed since my union membership fees were automatically deducted from my monthly paychecks. I was glad, though, on days when the union made a round of inspection around the market to make sure that workers worked the legal maximum hours and not more. On those days, I could go home early.

**The CALU was created in 1970 and functioned until its forced dissolution under the new military government in 1981. So you became a member when the union still had a legitimate standing.**

I was a mere member when the union was legal. I became an active part of the union after it became de-legalized. When I turned 18, I discovered a program that allowed each clothes shop to pick one of the employees and send him or her to a trade school. My boss thought I was a hard worker and recommended me for a trade school in Yeongdeungpo. Then my father suddenly passed away, and I had to work hard to support my family. So I let my *shida* go to school instead of me. I regretted this decision all my life and later enrolled in a night school. There were four night schools around my workplace at the time. Older girls who continued to work for the union after its dissolution were also clandestine links to these night schools. The people who played leading roles in these night schools finally stood up and organized a campaign in 1984 to restore the CALU. That was when I became a union executive.

**It must have been difficult to work full time and also support the union simultaneously.**

Yes, it was. So, after nine years of work and becoming a full-time labor union executive, I left the children's clothes factory I worked at. Our union was illegal at the time, so we could not collect membership fees. The core members decided to take turns to work and share their income with non-working executives.

**What was the most memorable part of your union experience?**

I still remember the strikes we held over wages. After working as a full-time executive for some time, I began to work again at a subcontractor factory for a children's clothes shop at Jongam-dong. There I worked, studied and debated with my coworkers and jotted down their complaints against the company. While struggling with workers' actual needs and conditions on field, I came to learn a lot about what it means to unionize and what it means to be part of workers' solidarity.

**You and I met in 1981, I remember? Didn't we meet at one of the union meetings after the CALU became de-legalized?**

Yes, that's right. We met at "Mother's Home" at Chang-dong. That was what we called the house where you and your mother, Yi So-sun, lived. The words "Chang-dong" and "Mother's Home" held special significance to us. That was where we gathered for our all-night-long meetings and education. We stayed up all night discussing and learning things and left early in the morning for work without getting a shut-eye. Looking back, I wonder where we found the strength to do that. But we did that for countless months and years until we regained a legitimate standing.

**Yes, those were the days of hard work by day and struggle by night. We went to jail quite often, too.**

That kind of life continued until 1987. We organized street campaigns almost every other day. We went around neighborhoods to post union campaigns and posters early in the morning so that workers could get a glimpse of them as they commuted to work. We had to take different routes to our meeting place every time to avoid possible tails. I discovered that there were police officers assigned to tailing me. Fortunately, I was never indicted in court, but I did get detained for three times, for 15 days in a row.

"*Of course I got afraid and worried while working for the union. But I never wanted to run away. When a problem happens, I actually get calm and brave.*"

**Weren't you scared? Didn't you ever want to run away?**

Of course I got afraid and worried while working for the union. But I never wanted to run away. When a problem happens, I actually get calm and brave.

# Another Obstacle: Living as a Woman in Korea

—

**When did you get married? I heard that you have had quite a marriage so far.**

I got married when I was 28 years old. We union women tended to get married much later than other women our age at the time because we were so busy with union work. Our male counterparts were equally busy with labor activism. As you know, my husband was a labor activist who quit university to find work as a factory worker and unionize fellow workers. When we got married, we were both factory workers, so I assumed that we would live the rest of our shared life as fellow workers. Three years after our wedding, though, my husband decided to go back to school. We lived in Anyang because he was working at a rack factory at the time. After he decided to return to university, we moved to Seoul to live with his parents.

**So that's how you came to live with your in-laws!**

My husband was the eldest son in his family. He was also the best student and went to university, so his entire family held him in such high regard and had many expectations of him. When I first went to meet with his parents, his mother told me that there were only three things she looked for in her daughter-in-law-to-be: a high school degree, a hometown anywhere in Korea but the Jeolla provinces, and a church-goer. I met none of these criteria. There were strong objections to our marriage, but I was already pregnant with our first

*"My life as a wife and mother involved far greater struggles than labor activism. In hindsight, I never took a break. I do not remember all the workplaces I worked at. I just kept working at whatever job was given to me."*

child, so what could they have done? So I lived a life of suffering at the hands of my in-laws for almost quarter of a century. That is why I could never let go of my work. I preferred working much more to staying at home.

**Did your husband help you at all?**

I thought I could live an entirely different life once my husband got his degree and found a well-paying job. He couldn't have done more to contradict my expectations, though. He had little knowledge of the real world, but set up his own business three times, all of which ended up in bankruptcy. I earned more than other women in my line of work, but could not save money because I had to repay his debts for two decades. After he found work as a paid employee about a decade ago, our living got a bit more stable.

**It must have been quite a struggle to raise a family and work full time.**

My life as a wife and mother involved far greater struggles than labor activism. In hindsight, I never took a break. I do not remember all the workplaces I worked at. I just kept working at whatever job was given to me. Until 10 years ago or so, I worked hard because that was the only way to raise and support my family. Now, I am glad that I have never given up on this work.

**You have lived such a hard and toilsome life, yet you seem so comfortable outwardly.**

I am upset about that myself. Yes, I have lived a life that required me to work constantly. But I never let it claim who I am. I am a born optimist and positive thinker. When people are faced with a difficult task or problem, they may ask whether they are up to it. I don't do that. I just start working on it. When anyone asks me to make clothes of a really particular and difficult design, I never wonder whether I could do it, but instead apply myself to it with full zeal. I think it is this optimism that has kept me going all these decades.

# Making the Clothes I Want, When I Want, with My Whole Heart

—

**How did you get started on making clothes using natural fabrics?**

At one point in my life, I wanted to do something I had never tried before. I wanted to do something that I could call my own and that I could really enjoy. About 10 years ago, someone introduced me to a natural-dye dressmaking shop at Insa-dong, so I learned this new craft there. My monthly pay was meager in comparison to what I was used to receive, but I enjoyed learning new things there.

**After working and learning there, you came to work with me and also began to teach your craft at the Korea Academy of Fashion and Sewing.**

That's right. I began to work in the social enterprise you created, and helped to set up fashion shows and enjoyed working there for about two years. I began to work at the Academy as an assistant instructor to help advanced-level students prepare for their fashion show. At the time, I was the only at the Academy with experience in natural-fabric dressmaking. So I began to teach the new class on natural fabrics that was created the following year.

**I hear you are quite popular among your students.**

I have taught over 200 students so far. I keep in touch with many of them. There are even groups of students that regularly meet and include me in their activities. I call them and they call me from time to time. We also use social media actively to keep in touch. I have a number of students who make a point of visiting me on Teachers Day every year. I love my job and helping my students.

**What's your plan for the future?**

"*Mere immersion is not enough. I really have to work at this as if my whole life depended on it. Consumers will know the difference in quality that this kind of effort makes.*"

I wish I could do something that I could call entirely my own. Right now, I have to make things as ordered by my clients. At some time in the future, though, I want to make my own clothes, creating the designs and finishing dressmaking all on my own. I think that I could get really immersed in my work when I create clothes of my own at my own pace instead of being forced to meet deadlines set by others.

**You have been teaching at the Academy for seven years now. Do you plan to continue in the future?**

Ever since I was a child, I have wanted to become a teacher. How rewarding is it to teach and help others? I will continue to teach as long as I can. Teaching two or three classes a week can amount to significant financial losses and wear me down at times. But I get more out of teaching than I give, so I cannot quit.

**We have talked quite a bit today, but the one thing I remember most is your expression of "wholehearted dressmaking."**

Dressmaking is a craft whose final products show how engaged and diligent I have been. Sometimes I get so many orders and forced to finish one order after another as soon as I can. My clients instantly tell the difference and call me back, asking me whether I was really the one who did the job. They know how much time I spend on each order because it shows in quality. That is why I have dedicated my whole heart to this craft. Mere immersion is not enough. I really have to work at this as if my whole life depended on it. Consumers will know the difference in quality that this kind of effort makes.

In Ji, I have met a lifetime friend and colleague who realized the importance of labor early on and waged her own struggles against an unjust world so that workers' rights would be respected and protected. As a woman, relatively uneducated, from a marginalized part of Korea and working in a lowly regarded line of work, Ji nonetheless continued her struggle to make the world better for herself and coworkers, and to find a profession she could dedicate herself to. She has worked tirelessly on improving her skills and is now recognized as a master of her field. The quality and beauty of the clothes she makes reflect her entire life and dignity as a human being.

The Clean Clothes Campaign (CCC) may not be a household name, but it is an international movement that seeks to raise the public awareness of the hardships and oppression with which Third-World women laborers struggle on a daily basis so as to pressure businesses into respecting workers' rights and improving working conditions. The label "CCC" is not given lightly to any beautiful and luxurious clothes. It is given only to products that were created in environments free of oppression and abuse. Master dressmakers can make clean and beautiful clothes only when their work is given due respect and recognition. Imagine clothes made by someone who is delighted and immersed in her work. Think of what great happy energy that clothes can give to the wearer.

*Making the clothes I want,*
*when I want,*
*with my whole heart.*

# I, Too, Would Like to Present "Made in Korea" Proudly to the World

Koh Mi-hwa (CEO, J Fashion)

As of 2013, it has been 15 years since I started running the company named J Fashion. The company got off to a successful start by specializing in the light manufacturing process of sewing pieces of lacework onto ankle-high stockings. We lost our clients, however, as Chinese manufacturers began to produce the same goods. For the next two years, we manufactured swimsuits, but this endeavor again ended in failure. It was around that time that we received our first order for footlets. While working on that order, we settled upon a brilliant idea about a new type of footlets, and began to manufacture and distribute them, which has since gone on to become a huge hit on the market. After years of struggle, J Fashion was finally resurrected. Given the explosive pace of growth in the orders we received, we began to divide our orders with small-scale factories in and around the town of Iksan, Jeollabuk-do.

After working on that arrangement for a while, we decided to expand our production and enter the Kaesong Industrial Park in North Korea. The escalating tension in South-North Korean relations, however, resulted in the temporary shutdown of the Park. We were then forced to relocate to Vietnam. Having opened a new factory in Vietnam in 2012, the number of employees it hires has increased to over 500 in just a year. We now produce over 1.5 million pairs of footlets there each month. J Fashion will transfer all the required manufacturing facilities and technologies to Vietnam in return for a percentage of the cost of producing footlets in that country.

## It Takes Constant Innovation to Remain Topnotch

J Fashion manufactures almost all the footlets one can find in large department stores across Korea today. Even footlets bearing the brand names of popular stocking companies are manufactured by J Fashion. J Fashion was the first in the world to create seamless and all-silicon-soled footlets that never slip off the feet and bring maximum comfort to the wearer. We have had huge success with these socks over the last decade, and mistakenly believed that we could keep doing the same thing over and over. Yet Chinese manufacturers soon began to copy our goods, meaning we were no longer the exclusive manufacturer of this innovative footwear any longer. In hindsight, I realize that we should have filed patent applications on our sock structure and design. I still regret the fact that we ended up only registering the footlet design. (These days, we file for patents on all the goods we design.)

Merely diversifying the outward appearance of socks is not enough to prevent counterfeiting. Having realized this, we researched and developed innovative product designs for two years. The latest footlets are made entirely of silicon. They are extremely comfortable and also perfectly fitting to any shoes so that they will never come off the wearer's feet unless the wearer takes them off. Footlets have become something of a must-have item for wearers of sneakers these days, so there is great demand for our products. We have manufactured 500,000 pairs already this year, which sold out almost instantly every time we released them on the market. The footlets we distributed to shops in Japan, for the first time this year, have sold out also, leading these shops to order a million more pairs, which we will have to supply by next March.

New product developments and designs are at the top of my priority list. Raw material, fabrics, intermediary items and designs are all important elements. Any quality issues in the fabrics can instantly catch the consumers' attention. We have recently developed a product that involves combining *hanji* with Spandex. In order to produce footlets of quality fabric and components at affordable prices, we have to search a wide range of manufacturers and suppliers and meet with everyone involved. We try to procure all the fabrics we need from domestic — that is, Korean — sources. For the intermediary items and components, however, we also travel frequently to China as our work involves making use of these things from numerous Chinese sources.

We also have to keep our price competitive with Chinese-made goods. For now, our prices remain in the competitive range, which is why Japanese buyers keep coming back to us. Aside from pricing, we also need to make sure that our goods are irreplaceable by anything else. We have successfully entered a market as large as Japan, but I still travel there frequently, as well as to China, Vietnam, and elsewhere to read the trends and analyze market reaction to our products. All these flights feel exhausting at times, but I cannot afford to feel tired and take a break. We may be the world's best producer of footlets, but that position is not guaranteed to be permanent.

At present, we produce only sample footlets at our factory in Iksan, Korea. There are 15 employees at this factory who daily create new samples and send them to overseas clients. Fortunately, our clients accept almost all of them immediately and place orders. This attests to the quality of the products and designs we develop. The number and size of orders for our products keep piling up day in and day out. I am still grateful for having happened upon a niche market that keeps bearing golden eggs for us.

### The Apparel Industry as a Major Source of New Jobs

We now produce much of our footlets in Vietnam, but the Korean town of Iksan used to be our headquarters in the past. I still recall the days when our factory there exclusively hired locals as employees. We recruited our workers from across entire apartment complexes and gathered them in a single building per complex to have them work together. Our division of labor was arranged in such a way that workers on each floor had a unique specialty. Each floor had about 30 workers or so, who were all very productive. For producing stockings, for instance, workers on one floor would work on overlocking only; workers on another floor would work on removing the seams; and workers on still another floor would specialize in still something else. Our workers were mostly housewives who preferred to work in the comfort of their or their friends' homes, so we needed not provide them with a separate workspace.

This system yielded thousands of pairs of stockings and footlets each day. A typical worker would earn KRW 70,000 to 80,000 a day, and a very productive one would earn KRW 100,000 a day. A friend of mine received KRW 25 per pair of footlets, and worked for over a decade, back-stitching 3,000 to 4,000 pairs a month. She raised a daughter to become a schoolteacher on that income. We hired more than 200 such women at the time, and I recall paying over KRW 150 million monthly as wages to them. We could not maintain this apartment-type factory system long, however, as complaints over noise kept growing. We were thus forced to relocate, first to Kaesong Industrial Park, and after its shutdown, to Vietnam.

I still wish I could resume and continue production in Korea. Businesses of comparable size keep relocating their production overseas, citing the rising cost of labor in Korea as the main reason. In reality, however, Korean workers do not cost much more than their overseas counterparts. I would bring production back to Korea if only a few conditions were satisfied. I am not asking the government much. All I ask is some help with improving the working conditions in this country. The government, for example, can help businesses like J Fashion to create a small workspace nearby large apartment complexes so that housewives can gather and work there. The government can subsidize our rents and utility bills, and we can always bring in new orders for the housewives working in such workspaces.

Housewives would indeed welcome such a chance to work, while still being able to care for their children while at work. Light manufacturing businesses like J Fashion also prefer this kind of arrangement over setting up bulky factory and office facilities far away from workers' homes. We generate a profit of barely KRW 100 per pair of footlets we manufacture in Vietnam now. If we were to give all our Vietnamese workers the four mandatory public insurance policies as we would be required to do in Korea, we would never be able to retain the competitive prices of our products. Housewives in Korea also need work more than the four mandatory public insurances. Our kind of work could also give a steady and reliable source of income to self-rehabilitating groups, who are currently forced to depend on work-free government aid. Our kind of work, moreover, can create new jobs for people living outside the Seoul-Gyeonggi region. The solution to our dying apparel industry can be as simple as this.

I truly believe that the future of the Korean economy lies in reviving our apparel industry. With more jobs for people, we will have greater income equality and social justice. Aren't these the ideals we strive to achieve for our country? The apparel industry is labor-intensive and therefore has a great potential for creating jobs. J Fashion is a small business, but we can always bring in and distribute work as long as the Korean government helps us to set up workspaces where willing and hardworking people could gather. We could also readjust our production cost so as to make reliable monthly living wages possible for our workers.

Such an arrangement — the government setting up workspaces and J Fashion bringing in work — would create jobs for local housewives while also allowing them to care for their children, strengthen the local economy, and enable J Fashion to manufacture and export goods bearing the label "Made in Korea." With this kind of arrangement, the Korean economy would soon begin to grow again, with enough jobs to benefit many.

### Footlets Made in Korea for the World

The management philosophy of J Fashion is extremely simple. Our motto is "Do your best." I wake up at four o'clock every morning and spend the early morning hours on developing new product designs. Whenever there is a new product development project in progress, I go to work at six in the morning and stay there well past midnight. The employees at J Fashion are very supportive of the various initiatives I attempt, and contribute their own ideas and insights.

J Fashion is praised for its human-centered management style. The four friends of mine who worked with me decades ago at a company called Taechang, and who left the company with me to co-found J Fashion, are still working with me today. One of these friends has traveled between Korea and Vietnam with me countless times, overseeing the company's technical and management matters. At J Fashion, we rarely force anyone out. We do not dismiss employees simply for being "less productive" than others. If an employee finds a better job, career, or lifetime opportunity and decides to leave, we do not pressure him or her to stay. If an employee who has left the company decides to return to us, we also gladly welcome him or her back.

There are about 40 people working at the factory at Iksan today. Every kimchi-making season at the start of the winter, we gather at the factory to make kimchi and share steamed pork together. As we are about to expand our production in Vietnam, things are much busier at J Fashion. Once our production settles and becomes stable, however, I would like to subsidize the college education costs of our employees' children. I myself come from a poor family and barely finished high school, so I know what substantial help it would be for our employees to receive financial aid for their children's college tuition.

My hands are always calloused because I spend hours every day working on new product designs. In order to find the footlet design that will never slip off the wearer's feet, I worked all day every day with silicon and glue, and accidentally burned my hands multiple times while working the iron. These difficulties, however, hardly matter to me. I am happiest and most comfortable when I am at work. Work fills me with new energy and hope every day. It is the most exciting and fun thing I could do and enjoy.

At a recent meeting with Japanese buyers, I was asked about my dream for J Fashion. My answer was to grow the company until it employs 10,000 people so that everyone in the world would own at least one pair of J Fashion's footlets. The demand for our footlets mostly comes from women today, but our goal is to persuade every man want to wear our footlets. My wish is to produce footlets, bearing the label "Made in Korea," for all consumers worldwide. My coworkers and I at J Fashion will continue to focus on footlets until that wish comes true.

**About Koh Mi-hwa**

Koh began working at an undershirt-manufacturing business named Taechang at age 19. In just one year, Koh was included in the select group of employees given advanced training, and worked at the company for 15 more years afterward. She left Taechang to start her own business, at first with only three sewing machines. Her business began by manufacturing stockings and made its mark on the market by producing mesh stockings with lacework bands. Now manufacturing footlets, socks and stockings, J Fashion is Korea's No. 1 manufacturer of footlets. The company has been granted multiple utility design and patent rights, and continues to research and develop new product designs. The company's own brands include Vernube, soksj, and Angel J.

---

## Symposium
## for future small urban manufacturers

# "I chose this way because I want to work as long as I wish to, drawing on my own skills."

Photo Caption: (From left to right) Lawmaker Chun Soon-ok; Yi Gyeong-ja, a graduate of the fashion sewing course at the Korean Advanced Sewing Skills Academy (KASSA), born in 1967; Hyeon Seung-tae, a graduate of the same course as Ms. Yi, born in 1986; Bak Yeong-hui, a student of the design technology course at KASSA, born in 1964; Na Hye-yeong, a graduate of the same course as Ms. Bak, born in 1969; Kim Yong-suk, a graduate of the fashion sewing course at KASSA, born in 1976; and Seo Ju-hyeon, a graduate of the computer-aided fashion design course at KASSA, born in 1969

**Date & Time** 7 p.m. March 5, 2015
**Venue** Conference Room, KASSA, 4th Floor, Seoul Design Support Center

**Chun, Soon-ok** I am really glad and grateful to meet all of you, future small urban manufacturers, in person. In 2013, I began interviewing artisans who had been making clothes, bags, jewelry and suits for decades. Every one of them is as precious as a pearl, but they were hidden beneath the earth for too long. Most of them worked hard their entire lives just to make ends meet, and they did not grumble when trampled on. I believe if we uncover these hidden pearls and string them onto a thread, we can make amazing jewelry with them. I decided to turn these interviews into a book, because I wanted to highlight that small urban manufacturing is not a sunset industry as is generally believed and highlight how hard they have worked to develop their skills to world-class standards even though they have been largely neglected and ignored by society and policy makers. Despite this, whenever I met them, the artisans expressed the same concern: the absence of the "next generation" who will take over from them. They say they need to pass on their skills before they reach an age when they can no longer work, but seldom do young people want to learn. I am keenly aware that without skilled young workers, there will be no future for the industry. Thus, I wanted to meet and see the "future" in person. In that vein, I've asked KASSA to convene a gathering of its students and graduates working in the field. So here we are today. I want to listen to why you first got into the industry, what visions you have and the like. This meeting is neither a serious debate nor a public hearing. Make yourself comfortable and talk to us as if you were at a pleasant gathering with friends or family [*Everyone laughs*].

**Chun, Soon-ok** Let's introduce ourselves in turn. I will start. My name is Chun, Soon-ok, and I am a lawmaker. I worked in small urban manufacturing in the Dongdaemun area for nearly two decades. Then, in 1989, I went to the UK and earned my doctorate. When I returned to Dongdaemun in 2001, I started working again as an assistant sewing machine operator in factories. While I was at the job, I began to look into the conditions of businesses in the Dongdaemun area. I visited factories and asked many questions to the ladies working there. They answered my questions, without even stopping their sewing machines. Despite this, they did not get pricked by the needle even once. [*Laughs*] So, I told them they are like Han, Seok-bong's mother, the famous woman in a Korean folk tale, who skillfully cut long, thin rice cakes into even slices in pitch darkness. I asked them whether it was not tough for them to work 13 or 14 hours a day. All of them said it was O.K. They said it was good to have skills. Then, I asked whether they were healthy, and they answered they were fine. But they usually took two or three different pills for hypertension and diabetes at least, claiming that no one is that healthy. Since I became a lawmaker in 2012, I have thought a lot about how to create a better environment for those struggling technicians with dreams and how to help them develop their skills to world-class standards. Today's meeting is an extension of my efforts.

## "Why we first set foot in this industry."

**Seo, Ju-hyeon** Until 34, I didn't know anything about my aptitudes. I didn't care too much about what I liked, what I wanted to do and what I would do for a living. Then by chance I learned how to sew, and decided that it should be my lifetime job. It didn't matter whether it was making or selling clothes… It took me a full decade to finally settle down in the industry. This might be the limit for married women. It is hard for them to immerse themselves in a single thing and, even if they wish to do so, there is no one to guide them. As a result, they simply stop learning a skill. However, KASSA wants to secure jobs for its trainees, so I think it is a good channel for us. In 2011, I studied computer-aided pattern design at KASSA, which got me a production management position in 2012. Then, after working two years at one place, I got a job doing the same thing with another company. There are many people who discovered their skills later in life only to give up because they could not find a way forward. Fortunately, I had a good opportunity, and I think I hit the jackpot.

**Chun, Soon-ok** What are the main items you make?

**Seo, Ju-hyeon** The company I work for specializes in uniforms for teams, groups and the military.

**Chun, Soon-ok** Could you please elaborate on production management. Are there any specific qualifications? For example, being skilled at sewing or the like?

**Seo, Ju-hyeon** The mass production of garments involves raw and subsidiary materials, factories to which work orders are to be placed, verification on whether the orders are correctly executed and whether the clothes are properly made, and delivery to the buyers. A production manager is responsible for the entire process. Though I've learned a lot about sewing, pattern and computer-aided design (CAD), I cannot say I am an expert. Whereas artisans or skilled technicians invest their time honing their skills through practice, I educated myself through books and working with mentors. Although I am not skilled in each and every process, I can manage production because I am proficient in the entire workflow.

**Chun, Soon-ok** What did you do previously?

**Seo, Ju-hyeon** Originally, I majored in Chinese literature at university. Upon graduation, I took an IT job. Then I got married and quit.

**Chun, Soon-ok** You said that you learned how to sew by chance. What was the occasion?

**Seo, Ju-hyeon** I wanted to dress up a room with curtains and decided to make them on my own, so I went somewhere to learn how. My weakness is that I cannot pay attention for a long time since I am full of curiosity and have many interests. But when I sat at the sewing machine, I never seemed to be bored even if I stayed up past 10 p.m., 11 p.m. or midnight. This is still the case even now. I never get bored. When I focus on clothes, it is a time devoted only to me. It is a time of merriment and happiness.

**Chun, Soon-ok** So you've got a sewing machine at home and began sewing different things?

**Seo, Ju-hyeon** Yes. While I was at it, I found out that there were patterns. I then learned about patterns and saw people designing patterns on the computer. So I learned about CADs. Actually, after learning how to sew, I worked in a market and as an assistant sewing machine operator as well. I would have become a skillful sewer if I had kept working for a decade. But, as I have a vast range of interests, I think my current job fits me perfectly. Since I manage the entire process, there is the right amount of variety as well.

**Kim, Yong-suk** In my case, my mother was a sewer who crafted traditional Korean costumes. It was only natural for me to learn from my mother how to operate the sewing machine to make those traditional garments. I was born in Cheongju but moved to Seoul for my husband. And I did not work for over a decade after my first baby was born. But, with three children, we desperately needed a second source of income. There were plenty of small factories around Myeonmok-dong where I live. As I was able to use the sewing machine, I thought that a little bit of learning would help me to land a job in such a factory. I learned about KASSA through the internet and, from June 2014, I enrolled in the fashion sewing course. Even though making a traditional Korean costume may sound difficult, it is quite simple. If you can operate a sewing machine, you can make it after only a little bit of learning. But, to me, making garments was a totally different experience. It was very tricky.

**Chun, Soon-ok** Where are you working now?

**Kim, Yong-suk** Fortunately, I caught the attention of the sewing master, Kim Do-yeong, and started studying under her in her workshop. Before I got married, I was confident with the sewing machine. But even if you complete a course at the academy, you cannot immediately work as a sewing machine operator. Even if you land a job through someone's recommendation, you may not be treated even as an assistant sewing machine operator and may simply be ignored. I've witnessed many such cases. But this did not happen to me. I really appreciated the chance to operate a sewing machine under a sewing master, and I think I am really lucky to have had the chance to learn significant clothing-making skills from her.

**Na, Hye-yeong** I became familiar with the sewing machine while expecting my first baby and had quit my job. Believing that it would have a good prenatal effect on the unborn baby, I decided to make swaddling clothes and diapers. So I bought a sewing machine. I'd already been sewing as a hobby for about a decade by the time I was 46. Back then, I was working in an office and thought I was close to my own limits. Although it was an acquaintance's company, I figured I had overstayed my welcome, so I thought it would be a good idea to acquire some skills. As I was not accustomed to the area, I decided to learn through books. I enrolled in the Clothing & Textiles Department at Korea National Open University. When it came to skills, KASSA seemed to be the best fit. I also read a news article about Jang Hyo-ung, a senior alumnus of my alma mater and a director at KASSA. Currently I study clothing design and production in the design technology course at the academy. KASSA got me a job at a hat-making company, but I quit after only four months. Originally I wanted to work in the garment industry, and hat-making appeared to be OK. But the job did not suit me, so I quit. It was too different from garment making. Currently, I am focusing only on learning.

**Chun, Soon-ok** No matter where you get a job, it takes at least three years for you to learn the skills you need to set up a business or to hatch a new plan.

**Na, Hye-yeong** You can say that again. However, at the moment, things are going as I desire. For example, last year I wanted to exhibit my creations, and KASSA put together an exhibition for us on April 16, 2015. After completing the course at KASSA last April, I planned to open a small workshop to sell small items, and now I am discussing it with a group of friends. Though I am not sure how that will turn out…

**Chun, Soon-ok** That's a wonderful idea.

**Bak, Yeong-hui** When I was in my 20s, I used to perform in theatrical shows. During this time, my interest in theatrical clothing grew. After married, my husband did not want me working outside the home. So I learned about it only as a hobby. When I began learning how to make traditional Korean clothing in 2011, I dreamt of making a variety of such clothing, creating a fusion of traditional and contemporary fashion. A fellow student with whom I had learned to make traditional clothing recommended KASSA to me. I finished the basic and advanced sewing courses, and am currently enrolled in the design technology course. Later I want to be a theatrical costume maker. What keeps me enthralled is the joy of meeting the audience through theatrical costumes and of creating a variety of artistic expressions. Needless to say, it is important to learn and refine your skills in the field. However, rather than mass-produced clothing, I want to make clothes that reflect a person's individuality.

**Chun, Soon-ok** Are you focusing only on learning?

**Bak, Yeong-hui** Outside the class, I currently work with the trainer Ms. Seong, Yeong-ja in her workshop, whom I met in the basic sewing course at KASSA. She said that classroom learning has a limit and that only hands-on experience in the field will create a real sense of what sewing is all about. She invited me to work for her on an hourly wage. Honestly, there were things I didn't know when I was learning. Field work seemed to be an insurmountable obstacle to me. I think I had confined myself within my own walls. But, when I actually began working, I was able to see how clothing was made and how the market worked. Age doesn't matter. At a glance, work experience appears to be vital in getting a job in the sewing industry. I think getting a job is not hard as long as you are willing to take any work, keep your eyes on the goal and persevere, and that can trump your lack of experience. Back when I was learning how to sew, I was shy and afraid that my age would prevent me from getting a job. Now, as I am in the field and exposing myself to the world, I feel my confidence coming back. I am enjoying my job right now.

**Hyeon, Seung-tae** I've always had a keen interest in fashion. Like most Korean men my age, I came across tailored suits for the first time in my life through a famous suit brand back then: Classico Italia. The classic Italian-style suits were popular in the Japanese market for over a decade, and arrived on the Korean market around 2007 or 2008. Around that time, there was a small community of people interested in Classico Italia suits. I was too young to wear deluxe tailored suits back then, so whenever we heard that some of the elder members of the community would get their suits tailored, myself and other guys would go to see the first fitting of a new suit at the tailor's. That's how we came across those suits. I was eager to learn how to make suits, but it was hard to find a place to learn. No university offered a suit-making course in their curriculum. Then I learned that there were two places teaching those skills. One was the

Tailor Academy run by Mr. Kim, Ui-gon, but by the time I came to know of it, the government subsidy to the academy had ceased. The other was an establishment run by the suit tailor Mun Byeong-ji. He'd made suits overseas for a long time and came back to Korea to teach his skills and arrange overseas jobs. It opened in Icheon, but closed after the first year. The government subsidy for that establishment discontinued as well because it failed to achieve its goal. Of the trainees, only two were eligible for U.S. visas, and the rest were employed within the country. Having missed those two opportunities, I began learning basic sewing skills here at KASSA for three months from June 2014. Upon completing the course, thanks to the help of Director Jang, Hyo-ung and Mr. Kim, Ui-gon, I got a job at a tailor's shop called "England." It is situated within the Renaissance Hotel, and I've been working there for three and a half months.

**Chun, Soon-ok** What did you do previously?

**Hyeon, Seung-tae** Originally I was working as a merchandiser doing shopping for others over two to three years. And, as a side job, I sold clothes and worked as a coordinator. The job goes like this: I would say to my clients, "You need a certain number of shirts and a certain number of trousers, but when I looked in your closet, I think you'll want to get rid of these and keep those," and at the end I would add, "I have white shirts you might like. The market price is this much but I can get them for you for half price." Most of them would buy it. [*Everyone laughs*]

**Chun, Soon-ok** A fashion coordinator is an important role. In the National Assembly, if I tell my colleague "That color suits you," it is a great compliment. Even though I'm not a fashionista, I can appreciate good fashion. I can feel that female lawmakers inwardly wait for my comments on their outfits, especially when they are specially adorned. From 2006, lawmakers began taking the stage in the Suda Gongbang Fashion Show, and they liked it a lot. I think fashion coordinating is an up-and-coming job. There are some affluent people who find it difficult to pull together a stylish look. And not a small number of people say that shopping is tiresome and very time consuming.

**Yi, Gyeong-ja** In my case, I did mostly office jobs. But, after getting married, it was difficult for me to get a job. While caring for my children, I made accessories on the side. I was exhausted and the money wasn't good. I could not even take care of my children. Then I tried this and that until one of my friends asked me to work for the business management team of an IT company. Several years later, the company I worked for merged with another company, and a year later I was laid off. I guess it was because of my age… Anyway, before leaving the job, l learned many things as hobbies because I liked to learn. However, after leaving the workplace, turning hobbies into a job is easier said than done. Anyway, immediately before joining the company, I learned how to design traditional Korean clothing at Seoul Institute of Technology & Education, at the Jungbu Campus in Hannam-dong. Back then, for the first time in my life, I ran a sewing machine, and learned about sewing patterns. It felt like a new world. But completion of the course was not enough for me to land a job. Then, one of the instructors found a job for me in a shop in Gwangjang Market. They asked me to work as an assistant operator for three years, with no pay for the first year…

**Chun, Soon-ok** That is the so-called "passion pay," the exploitation of inexperienced workers.

**Yi, Gyeong-ja** Yes, that's correct. They said "What you've learned from the institute is totally different from what we're doing in the market. If you learn skills here and become familiar with working with us over the first year, then we will pay what we see as appropriate. Then, after three years, we will provide you with work." How could I hold out in that job for three years? Money is required to sustain life. Then, one of my fellow graduates introduced me to KASSA, and I finished the fashion sewing course in 2014. For two weeks last September, I received on-the-job training at an establishment in Changsin-dong. The training was intense but I learned plenty along the way. I had to stand on my feet for 12 hours a day, from 9 a.m. to 9 p.m. Although they were considerate towards trainees, I couldn't sit idle when others were busy. So, I cut thread all day long with a thread clipper. That was when I realized how poor the working conditions are in the sewing industry. I finished the academy but could not find a job. So, I practically begged the instructor, Kim, Do-yeong, to give me a job. I told her, "I do not mind working without pay as long as I can work and learn." But she told me, "That is not acceptable. You need some money to sustain yourself." So, I am now working for her and receiving some pay on a wage.

## "We need the strength to hold out."

———

**Chun, Soon-ok** In this era of aging populations and insecure employment, the greatest hope and vision for the future lies in learning some skills. The only thing that matters is how well you can develop your skills. No matter whether you start your own business or work with others, opportunities will surely come in your life. In that regard, I think that all of you made the right choice. Especially you, Mr. Hyeon. It is highly commendable that you thought of learning these skills at your young age.

**Hyeon, Seung-tae** I have no one to rely on. My family is poor and there are other difficulties. Under the circumstances, even if I choose an office job, it would not be an easy feat. Taking all these things into account, I thought it would be better to choose this path. I like this sort of work. It takes a super long time to develop advanced skills, and one day I might regret taking this career path, but I think it's better to start now.

**Chun, Soon-ok** Before I came here today, I went to Sinjeong-dong and Sinwol-dong, Yangcheon-gu. There are many bag makers there. At one of the factories, I saw a couple, their two sons, the woman's sister and her son working together. The two sons were in their 20s and were good-looking like movie stars. The working conditions were poor since it was a factory in the basement. Regardless of these conditions, they were running their sewing machines without complaints. So, I asked them why they were there. They said, "If we want to get an average, run-of-the-mill company job, we may waste time by writing and putting in applications here and there. And, despite all those efforts, we may still end up getting only a temporary or contract job. However, if we work here, things will get better as time goes on. We think this is a better way." So, I gave them the thumbs up.

**Hyeon, Seung-tae** If you learn a skill, you can open a business with very little money. That's the advantage.

**Chun, Soon-ok** Although small-scale merchants and manufacturers are collectively referred to as "small enterprises," small merchants and sole proprietors usually call it quits within three years of opening their franchises or restaurants. This may be attributable to their lack of skill. In contrast, the average small urban manufacturer or SUM stays in business for at least a decade, in most cases, for nearly two decades. That is the case even for ultra small manufacturers in Changsin-dong. When I left for the UK in 2001, SUMs talked about the shortage of work. Even now, they still express concern over the shortage of work. But they stay afloat. While it may feel difficult now, if you persevere through the first two to three years, your confidence as a technician will grow. You made a choice. No one forced you. However, even if you've decided to pursue it in earnest, you may have some concerns. Let's talk about them.

**Hyeon, Seung-tae** Above all, my biggest concern is money. Most people my age, who are interested in suit making, came into the industry between 2007 or 2010 at the latest. However, they often quit because the pay is too low. Those who come to Seoul from rural areas or small towns and graduate from a college or fashion academy, they get a job and keep it for a year. However, they cannot earn enough to support themselves, not to mention give a little to their families. So they find another job.

**Bak, Yeong-hui** Even if you are skilled, you cannot hold out without some strength. Given my age, I am not as fearless as those young people. If I make the wrong choice, it may last until the end of my life. So, I have more to think about. I was at a crossroads. I was faced with two choices — traditional Korean clothing or contemporary fashion. To me, contemporary fashion was too diverse and complex. I was uncertain whether I could persevere. So, the idea of making traditional clothing was tempting: if you can operate a sewing machine, it takes only a little training to attain a certain level. You can reach it in a relatively short time. You can be a designer of traditional Korean clothing with only a third of the effort to become a contemporary fashion designer. Moreover, since few people want to go into the traditional Korean clothing industry, teachers are more willing to pass on their brand name to their students. In contrast, many contemporary fashion designers start at a young age and study overseas. Thus, in practicality, it is hard to persevere. It was due to those circumstances that I had a great deal of misgivings.

**Seo, Ju-hyeon** The company I work for manages six or seven factories where the aging of the work force is the most serious concern. Whenever I visit one of them, I feel that the most urgent task is to groom the next generation of skilled young people, unless the government regards sewing as a sunset industry and is unwilling to provide assistance. When interns join the factory, there should be some incentive, whether a bright outlook or enough money, so that they can stay onboard after the completion of their internship program. I am working in the field, but I cannot see any such thing.

**Kim, Yong-suk** To me, child-rearing was and is the primary concern. For the past month, I have been working overtime every day. Work finishes at 11 p.m. and I come home around midnight. One of my kids is currently enrolled in a daycare center, and another is in elementary school. My mother-in-law picks up the kids from the daycare center and the school and drops them off at home. Then, my husband takes care of them after work. The government encourages families to have more children and says that it will provide assistance. But I see no practical implications. We have to pick the kids up at the day care center no later than 7 p.m. And the elementary school provides child care service until 8 or 9 p.m. but with limited accommodation. They ask us to submit a certificate of employment, without which we are not eligible for the service. In some workplaces, it is difficult to obtain a document verifying our employment. Even in the case of the childcare service offered by the local community, there are more than 100 or 200 children on the waiting list. They say that the aging of the work force is a huge problem in the sewing industry. But to be more exact, it is only after a certain age that one can enter the workforce. I became more acutely aware of that. I have three children and they are still young. So, at the moment, we can sustain ourselves even if my husband is our only source of income. But as our kids grow up, I need to work to cover our expenses. I decided to try working two or three years in the sewing industry before we have to spend more money on our kids. I want to keep working, but I see my husband and mother-in-law growing tired and burning out from the kids.

**Seo, Ju-hyeon** That's where you need to be patient.

**Kim, Yong-suk** I am already being patient, honestly. [*Everyone laughs*] I always tell myself "It'll be better once I overcome this one hurdle." But, it's really tough. Companies in other industries have specific work hours and maternity leave policies. But such things are out of the question in sewing operations. Your employer asks you to work overtime, and you say you can't because of the kids. Then the boss fires you. All of the factories boast that 71-year-old grandmothers are on their payroll. That's what they're proud of. That is the truth. But in order for the young people to learn and work in this field, measures need to be taken to help them in the struggle of trying to work while taking care of their kids at the same time.

**Bak, Yeong-hui** Isn't it possible for factories to run two or three shifts a day or weekend shifts?

**Chun, Soon-ok** No, in reality, small factories cannot do so. As you may know the workflow at sewing factories peaks at 7 or 8 p.m. These are the most productive hours. Work usually ends at 11 p.m. It's a pity but productivity would not pick up if work ended at 7 p.m.

**Kim, Yong-suk** Ms. Kim Do-yeong's workshop runs a piecework system, which means relatively flexible working hours. So, on a usual day, I send my husband to work and kids to school by 9:30 a.m. and then I myself go to work. However, even under the flexible working hour system, I need to finish my assignment by the due date and time. You cannot arbitrarily move the deadline on the grounds of personal circumstances.

**Seo, Ju-hyeon** Is it tailoring or making the whole garment on your own?

**Kim, Yong-suk** It's not a tailoring shop but a small order manufacturing operation. Ms. Kim cuts the cloth, and then I do the rest.

**Chun, Soon-ok** The way I see it, you are quite skillful. What are the main items?

**Kim, Yong-suk** Skirts, dresses, jackets, T-shirts and everything else. [*All in awe*]

**Chun, Soon-ok** This means you are really highly-skilled. You can sew anything to order, so you don't run out of work.

**Yi, Gyeong-ja** I work in the same workshop as her. But she has run a sewing machine for over a decade. So the difference between me and skilled operators like her is the difference between sky and earth. As a late starter, my 'wants' are far ahead of my skills.

**Chun, Soon-ok** Skills will improve as time goes on if you work on it every day. They will surely get better.

**Yi, Gyeong-ja** Ms. Kim Do-yeong said so as well, "Time will take your frustration away."

**Chun, Soon-ok** If you learn skills in that manner, you can work in the industry for the next two decades at least. Most sewing machine operators I know say, "I will work until I have to wear magnifying glasses to thread the needle." I believe you will do so.

**Seo, Ju-hyeon** I've seen 70-year-old hand sewers sewing on the finishing touches.

**Chun, Soon-ok** In the place I visited today, I saw an 80-year-old hand sewer. She looked surprisingly young, maybe because she has continued working.

**Seo, Ju-hyeon** Indeed, there seems to be no retirement age in the sewing industry. It is not idle talk to say if you can walk on your feet and thread a needle, you can continue sewing.

# "If you have skills, so many doors are open to you."

——

**Chun, Soon-ok** Each of you decided to enter this industry when you were in your early or mid 40s, except you, Mr. Hyeon. [*Everyone laughs*] I guess the biggest reason for your choice is that you can work into your old age. Correct?

**Bak, Yeong-hui** Yes. After getting married, I was unemployed for some time. I worried about my living situation in my old age and pondered what I should do. Then it just finally became clear that skills are the answer. I learned about hairdressing but it didn't suit me. But, regarding sewing, I have memories of when I was young and off school, making doll clothes. Learning how to sew at the academy rekindled my memory of that experience. Also, I wanted to work into my old age.

**Seo, Ju-hyeon** I have five certificates: Cooking, baking and others. I've learned many things with all of them. But, they didn't seem to be right for me. I feel certain that my aptitude lies in sewing.

**Chun, Soon-ok** I can see the satisfaction on your face.

**Seo, Ju-hyeon** The workload is heavy but I am satisfied with my work. It is true that sometimes I think I might die from the workload and, at times, it feels like there is no time to breathe. When I was a novice, the pay was negligible. I began production management in 2005. The starting monthly salary was KRW 800,000. Then, KASSA got me a job paying KRW 1 million per month. When the factory was busy, I had to work past 11 p.m. or midnight, and sometimes on weekends. But I really liked working. At work, you face crisis or limits at some point. What enables you to overcome these obstacles can be money or people. In my case, the enabler was the president of the factory. He raised my monthly salary from KRW 1 million to 1.2 million on the grounds of seniority. Though I am interested in fashion, I am old and cannot compete with young people as far as fashion sense goes. So, my weapon is dedication and perseverance. For instance, when my company received an order for a product planned in Japan, I roamed around the Dongdaemun area for more than five hours a day, looking for the most similar fabric to that of the desired product and finally found it. My heels got plantar fasciitis after that.

**Chun, Soon-ok** When did you especially feel limits?

**Seo, Ju-hyeon** When I say limits, I mean mistakes. For example, there were some instances where I chose B instead of A, which prevented us from delivering the product on time, causing loss to the president. When that happened, I just wanted to crawl into a hole or quit my job. But, the president intentionally overlooked it. So, I've worked for him for a long time. When you make a mistake, a word of encouragement or criticism from your boss makes a huge difference. Just having someone who tells you that all will be well can be of great help. Even now, I keep hitting those limits. But I persevere, thinking that once I quit, I will not be able to get to the next stage. I will be in my 50s soon. I hold out thinking that I should keep working until at least 50.

**Chun, Soon-ok** What do you want to do after you turn 50?

**Seo, Ju-hyeon** Initially, I wanted to sell clothes under my own brand name. But when I thought about the practicality of it, it felt like a far-fetched dream given my knowhow and financial situation. So I shelved the idea. My final goal is to open a workshop around Jiri Mountain.

**Hyeon, Seung-tae** If you have financial freedom, it's nice to do what you want to do.

**Seo, Ju-hyeon** Probably, I will not be able to achieve financial freedom even by then. I just want to make clothes for the villagers in exchange for potatoes or the like. Until then, I will just continue working. But it is neither to earn money nor gain work experience. I cannot quit my job because I am afraid of being unemployed.

**Chun, Soon-ok** All in all, you've chosen this job because you believe these skills will enable you to work into old age. Correct?

**Bak, Yeong-hui** Yes. I hope I can use my skills and work into my old age, having to please others and being discriminated against because of age or other reasons.

**Kim, Yong-suk** When I look around where I live, I see many sewing factories thrive. They are partially specialized, in button-hole punching, back-stitching on the sleeves and hem stitching and so on. All of them are in good shape. Of course, it is better to set up a large establishment. But, it doesn't need to be big or have lots of equipment. It is sufficient to have a sewing machine in a place where you want and to use your own skills. The charm of this industry is that all possibilities are open. I am now making garments, but someday I think I can push my boundaries by learning more about cloth-cutting and pattern designing. I will work and improve on my skills further. From there I am sure I will find the best way for me. In other areas, it is difficult for a 40-year-old woman to start over. However, in the sewing industry, 40 years is not that old… [*Everyone laughs*] Here, I feel like I can do anything. My dreams are growing, and I expect I will achieve much more in the future than I have done so far.

## Gap between Technical Training And Actual Practice in the Field

——

**Chun, Soon-ok** As a graduate of KASSA, what do you think is the biggest difference between what you learned in class and what you do in practice? Or, to put it another way, what is the greatest difference between expectations and reality?

**Kim, Yong-suk** In job interviews at factories, if the interviewer asks what you want to do in the factory, most of the interviewees reply that they want to be a sewing machine operator. There are that many people who want that job. So, the interviewer says, "Why does everyone want to be a sewing machine operator? An assistant sewing machine operator is a good position to start with." In my own head I think, "I learned how to operate a sewing machine, then it is only natural for me to operate a machine." But, the reality is far from what I envisioned. Previously, when I went to thread shops to buy subsidiary materials that I would use in on-the-job training, shopkeepers there told me, "Training at an academy serves no purpose. Even if you finish the course, no one will hire you or even recognize your skills." They said, "Rather than learning in an academy, it is better to be an assistant sewing machine operator in a factory. It is a faster way to develop your skills." I didn't believe them. When I finally began to look for work, the reality was just as they told me. People didn't recognize the skills I had learned. This hit home when I began working in Ms. Kim Do-yeong's workshop. Honestly there is no way 3 months of training can lead you to a sewing machine operator job in the field.

**Seo, Ju-hyeon** You took the words right out of my mouth. Unless the training period is extended to three years...

**Kim, Yong-suk** At the beginning, everybody comes to the academy thinking that they can be a sewing machine operator once they finish the course. However, when they come back from on-the-job training, they say, "Ah, this is not for me," and leave. [*Whispering and expressed agreement*]

**Chun, Soon-ok** Are there really so many trainees who give up after field training?

**Kim, Yong-suk** Yes. As far as I know, few remain in the industry.

**Chun, Soon-ok** Of all the graduates in a class, how many trainees end up working in the field?

**Yi, Gyeong-ja** Twenty trainees form a class. But just a few, about 10 percent will work in the industry. In my class, Ms. Kim Yong-suk and I are the only ones working in the field. We are not sure if we know all those who are not working. But, a high estimate is maybe 5 people. Others do the training and then give up.

**Chun, Soon-ok** After finishing the entire course at the academy, they just give up during the two-week field training?

**Kim, Yong-suk** Yes. That's because what they face in reality differs from what they have heard. Factories accept trainees because they can claim a grant. But, since trainees are not familiar with the job, they are of no help. Factories are so busy processing orders that they have no time to teach skills. So they leave trainees unattended. It doesn't matter whether the trainees sit idle or develop their skills by mimicking what they see in the factory. Two weeks will fly by anyway. As a result, a quick-witted person may last longer but most trainees will reach their limit.

**Bak, Yeong-hui** Companies just complain about the shortage of skilled workers. However, I think it is necessary to foster links between training institutes and the industry.

**Kim, Yong-suk** First of all, I think it is better to learn sewing skills at a big factory with more than 20 employees. If we learn what we've learned at the academy in a well-equipped place and the factory teaches us those skills in exchange for a grant for two to three months, they may hire us to prevent their efforts from being wasted.

**Seo, Ju-hyeon** But your idea is not without limitations. Factories cannot teach you how to operate a sewing machine.

**Hyeon, Seung-tae** Because they have to use the sewing machines to churn out products…

**Seo, Ju-hyeon** Yes, time is money. Assistant sewing machine operators are the only people who can be trained at the factory. But assistants also cost money. Thus, it is practically impossible to implement such a training regime at a factory.

**Kim, Yong-suk** Factories are unwilling to hire recent graduates of a sewing academy without work experience. In contrast, they impart training to those who have two or three years of experience as an assistant sewing machine operator to turn them into sewing machine operators. Even though they say they have no time to educate trainees, it's clear that they are not that time-constrained.

**Seo, Ju-hyeon** I think it would be better if the training period at this sort of training institute were three years, not three months. Three years of training would be enough for us to be accepted as sewing machine operators.

**Hyeon, Seung-tae** If it is a full-time training course, two years would suffice.

**Kim, Yong-suk** At KASSA, the training period is as short as three months. Making matters worse, classes are only on Monday, Tuesday and Wednesday, and we are off for the rest of the week. During the four off-days, students usually forget what they have learned. Afterwards, they will insert the needle backwards… As a result, they cannot become fully proficient in sewing machine operation. Honestly, you cannot be hired after just three months of training, because you lack the necessary skills.

**Hyeon, Seung-tae** That was the case with the tailoring schools subsidized by the government. During the first one or two years, the training period was as long as six months from what I remember. But due to practical issues such as grants, it got shortened to three months. So the teachers there told us that it's a woefully slapdash training.

**Kim, Yong-suk** You cannot land a job even if you receive training at an institute, so you try yet another training program, but you are not still employed. I saw many people just doing more and more training.

**Chun, Soon-ok** So, what you are saying is that it is necessary to train an immediately productive workforce, correct? It's only when we can bring up trainees to that level that factories will willingly hire them. But it takes a long time for a trainee to reach that level, so the government offers grants…

**Kim, Yong-suk** A full overhaul might be difficult, but when it comes to the immediately productive workforce, I think a little change in the current system can be possible. For example, as the training period is short, the academy should focus only on a single skill so that the trainees can be fully proficient at that skill. Under the current system, even if trainees learn how to make, say, skirts, at the beginning of a course, they cannot make even the easiest skirt at the end of the course. That's because their memory fades while they learn to make trousers and other items. The ability to operate a sewing machine itself cannot land you a job.

**Bak, Yeong-hui** My opinions are a little different. For those individuals who cannot attend the entire week, the current system is good enough. It's totally useless without aspiring students.

**Seo, Ju-hyeon** So, I think we should try to change in order to give trainees more options. When I've mentioned "the next generation," I mean that the academy should offer its trainees sufficient education, even if it takes two years, so that trainees can be sure that, once they are trained at the academy, they can have the skills for a lifetime job.

**Bak, Yeong-hui** Another important problem lies in the ludicrously low unit prices that factories offer. Buyers pay a per-piece price, so the prices are dirt cheap compared to the final sales price. Seasoned veterans of the industry with decades of experience can easily get over it, but it's an uphill struggle for newcomers. So people are unwilling to take this job. Given a choice between factory work and an office job, it's no doubt that they will choose comfort in office buildings. You may put the blame on it being a 3D job, which stands for dirty, dangerous and demeaning. But, if they can receive fair compensation for their work, they would not be so hesitant. I am a bit incensed at the fact that, while one side reaps exorbitant profits, the other side cannot assert their full rights. If only people who make more effort can receive more rewards... If only they can develop a belief that they can get fair compensation for their work... It would be much better.

## Skills Are the Answer
——

**Chun, Soon-ok** Lastly, I'd like to ask what your final goal is. The answers can be inferred from the reasons why you first got involved in the industry. But, I want to know specifically what your goals, dreams and hopes are.

**Seo, Ju-hyeon** As I've mentioned earlier, mine is to open a workshop around Jiri Mountain, together with a community where people with diverse skill sets are gathered together and live... Until then, I will continue doing what I am doing, regardless of money or work experience.

**Kim, Yong-suk** I am not ready to dream about my old age. As of now, I am just determined to perfect these skills. My goal in ten years is to develop my skills to the extent that I can complete any given item without anyone's help.

**Na, Hye-yeong** I have plans but how they will turn out, who knows? Largely, the plan is to set up tailor-made clothing branches at hypermarkets across the country. I need a minimum of KRW 25 million in start-up money. There is a "Clo 3D virtual garment simulation system" with which you can design and sew a garment, fit it to a person and even test the fabric texture. It costs KRW 18 million and, in addition, I need to buy sewing machines and sergers which will cost several million won more. To earn this start-up money, I need to get a job and develop the skills required for the business for two to three years. I believe something will come out of this plan in ten years.

**Chun, Soon-ok** Setting up branches in hypermarkets means that you want to sell tailor-made clothes at prices affordable to the public. At similar prices to off-the-rack garments?

**Na, Hye-yeong** Yes. When you go to a large store, you buy not only groceries but also clothes. My father has long arms, my brother is burly, and some other family members are short. They ask me to tailor clothes for them, if I can. If tailored clothes are not pricey, who wouldn't want to buy clothes tailor-made for them?

**Bak, Yeong-hui** I like stages and want to make theatrical clothing. Only with those items, it will not be enough to pay the bills. So I want to make tailored celebrity clothing as well. For celebrities who are eager to express their individuality, I will offer styles that suit each person specifically. I have connections and sales channels but, previously, I was not confident enough. I am looking for colleagues who can work with me after I receive orders from clients. It's OK even if they have not perfected their skills. Rather than hiring them as employees, I am considering working in a joint studio where individuals work with their own brand. If each can bring their own strengths and individuality, I believe we can meet diverse design needs.

**Hyeon, Seung-tae** I'm still a newbie so I want people to say things like, "He is a reliable sewer who can make what I want," as soon as possible. Then I can move to the next step. To be sure, someday I want to open a sewing factory or reap commercial success under my own brand…

**Yi, Gyeong-ja** My immediate objective is to learn skills as soon as possible, within a year, and persevere for three years. While I am at it, I might encounter challenging circumstances or hardships. But what I worry most about is my physical strength. So, my strategy is "Above all, persevere." [*Everyone laughs*] Therefore, as Ms. Kim Yong-suk said, I want to improve my skills to the degree that I no longer look to others while making any given item and then create a garment from start to finish. In addition, like Ms. Seo Ju-hyeon, I am quite interested in communities and sharing. I also think how wonderful it would be to share my skills with others, like Ms. Kim Do-yeong does. It's not easy but sounds very pleasant. What has surprised me most at KASSA is how much the trainers are willing to share their knowhow.

**Chun, Soon-ok** It was a pleasure to listen to your vivid and frank stories, penetrating advice and wonderful dreams. I had high expectations about who will come today and, after listening to what you have said, I find that you are deep in thought yet strong-willed. I am sure that you are well-qualified to be future small urban manufacturers. Once the Special Act on Support for Small Urban Manufactures comes into effect at the end of May, solutions will start to flow one by one for the many problems you have pointed out. I will strive to do that. If you have any questions or need information when you move forward with your plans and dreams, please do not hesitate to contact my office. I will advise you of what supportive measures, start-up funds and grants are available and where you can get help if you face difficulties in preparing documents or need consultation.

**Bak, Yeong-hui** Can we get support if several people get together to start a business?

**Chun, Soon-ok** Yes, of course. A business cooperative is entitled to receive up to KRW 100 million in grants from the Small and Medium Business Administration. A case in point is the handcrafted shoemakers' cooperative where makers, planners, former KAIST professors and accountants have joined together. They pooled together their individual talents and planned a business cooperative. With a grant of KRW 100 million, they bought the necessary machinery and facilities. Previously, when I checked with the Parliamentary Budget Committee, KRW 20.4 billion was earmarked for that purpose. But it targets only small merchants, and SUMs were not included. Initially, they supported mom-and-pop supermarkets, so called "Nadeul Stores", situated in traditional markets. But it didn't take off. So I proposed to use the funds as grants for SUMs.

**Bak, Yeong-hui** However, when applying for government grants, it is necessary to prepare more than 20 pages in documents, and it's very tricky.

**Chun, Soon-ok** In such cases, you can get help from experts who give consultations for free. Indeed, I've coordinated a meeting between bag makers in Jungnang-gu and some consultants, and they are working together now. Sometimes people do not know or find it difficult, but there are always alternative method which can help you achieve your goal. Bearing that in mind, I hope you overcome your difficulties. My philosophy is that "labor is the solution, and the solution is in the field." For you, I want to paraphrase that as follows: "Skills are the solution, and the solution can be found within your skills." I believe that skills will never betray you. Thank you for the lengthy time you have spent at this symposium. I sincerely hope to see you again.

# The full text of the 'Special Act on Support for Small Urban Manufacturers'

# Special Act on Support for Small Urban Manufacturers

[Enforced on May 29, 2015] [Enacted on May 28, 2014 by Act No. 12695]

## Chapter 1 Generals

Article 1 Purpose

The purpose of this Act is to contribute to the development of the national economy by establishing a system to support growth and development of small urban manufacturers and promoting their economic activities.

Article 2 Definitions

*Terms used herein are defined as follows: <Amended on January 28, 2015>*

1. The term, 'small urban manufacturer' means a person that satisfies each of the following requirements:

(a) Microenterprises as provided in Article 2 of the Act on Protection and Support of Microenterprises; and

(b) Entities in the highly labor-intensive, skill-based and cluster-forming manufacturing industry that mainly engage in a line of business prescribed by Presidential Decree.

2. The term, 'small urban manufacturer cluster' means an area which forms a cluster of small urban manufacturers' places of business (limited to those including manufacturing facilities such as machinery and equipment) in excess of the number prescribed by Presidential Decree for each administrative zone and which is designated in accordance with Article 15 hereof.

Article 3 Duties of Central and Local Governments

(1) The central government shall formulate and implement comprehensive policies to support small urban manufacturers.

(2) A local government shall formulate and implement policies to support small urban manufacturers in consideration of the central government's policies and regional characteristics.

Article 4 Relations with Other Laws

With respect to support for small urban manufacturers, this Act shall prevail over other laws.

## Chapter 2 Formulation and Execution of Plans to Support Small Urban Manufacturers

Article 5 Formulation of Comprehensive Plan to Support Small Urban Manufacturers

(1) The administrator of the Small and Medium Business Administration (SMBA) shall formulate a comprehensive plan to support small urban manufacturers (hereinafter referred to as "comprehensive plan") every five years in order to promote their growth and development.

(2) A comprehensive plan shall include each of the following:

1. Basic goals and direction of growth and development of small urban manufacturers;

2. Improvement of systems and laws regarding small urban manufacturers;

3. Matters related to utilization and transfer of skills of small urban manufacturers;

4. Matters related to training and supply of workers for small urban manufacturers;

5. Matters related to technology dissemination, innovation, and advancement for small urban manufacturers;

6. Matters related to support for domestic and foreign market development for products of small urban manufacturers;

7. Matters related to support for small urban manufacturer clusters; and

8. Other matters necessary to support small urban manufacturers.

(3) Necessary matters regarding the procedures and methods to formulate a comprehensive plan shall be prescribed by Presidential Decree.

Article 6 Formulation of Implementation Plan to Support Small Urban Manufacturers

(1) In order to pursue a comprehensive plan, the SMBA administrator shall formulate an annual implementation plan to support small urban manufacturers (hereinafter referred to as "implementation plan") in consultation with the heads of the central administrative agencies concerned.

(2) In an effort to support small urban manufacturers, the SMBA administrator may request the mayors of metropolitan cities and a metropolitan autonomous city and the governors of a special self-governing province and provinces (hereinafter referred to as "metropolitan city mayors and provincial governors") to take measures necessary to pursue an implementation plan.

(3) Necessary matters regarding formulation and pursuit of an implementation plan shall be prescribed by Presidential Decree.

Article 7 Statistical Data Investigation, etc.

(1) The SMBA administrator may collect, prepare, analyze, and manage statistical data concerning domestic and foreign small urban manufacturers necessary for a comprehensive plan and an implementation plan.

(2) For the purpose of collecting, preparing, analyzing, and managing statistical data as provided in the foregoing Paragraph (1), the SMBA administrator may request the heads of the local governments and public institutions concerned, small urban manufacturers, and appropriate institutions and organizations to provide necessary data and information.

(3) The SMBA administrator may commission specialized institutions to perform all or a part of the collection, preparation, analysis, and management of statistical data under the foregoing Paragraph (1).

## Chapter 3 Fosterage of Small Urban Manufacturers and Advancement of Their Skills

Article 8 Fosterage of Small Urban Manufacturers and Procurement of Human Resources

(1) The central government shall endeavor to foster small urban manufacturers and secure human resources for them.

(2) The central government may engage in any of the following undertakings to help small urban manufacturers secure high-quality human resources:

1. Training for acquisition and advancement of skills by small urban manufacturers;

2. Undertakings to promote inflow of new human resources and ensure employment stabilization;

3. Undertakings to promote welfare of workers of small urban manufacturers including rendering them better treatment;

4. Support for increased employment of unemployed youths as provided in Subparagraph 1, Article 2 of the Special Act on the Promotion of Youth Employment; or

5. Undertakings to support skills acquisition and reemployment of resignees or retirees.

Article 9 Management Guidance and Technology Development Support for Small Urban Manufacturers

(1) The SMBA administrator shall endeavor to provide management guidance to small urban manufacturers and to support their technology development.

(2) For the purpose of management guidance and technology development of small urban manufacturers, the SMBA administrator may provide support for any of the following undertakings:

1. Planning, development, and research of small urban manufacturers' business;

2. Counseling, guidance, and information provision to improve small urban manufacturers' management ability and technological level;

3. Technology innovation and development of small urban manufacturers; or

4. Research and studies necessary to enhance small urban manufacturers' technological and production ability.

Article 10 Designation of Technical Education and Training Institutes

(1) For the purpose of technology transfer and advancement by small urban manufacturers, the SMBA administrator may designate any of the following entities as a technical education and training institute:

1. High schools that use curricula customized for industrial needs or focused on experience in accordance with the Elementary and Secondary Education Act;

2. Universities, industrial colleges, junior colleges, and technical colleges under the Higher Education Act and polytechnic colleges under the Act on the Development of Workplace Skills of Workers;

3. Korea Institute of Industrial Technology under Article 8(1) of the Act on the Establishment, Operation and Fostering of Government-Funded Science and Technology Research Institutes; or

4. Other education and training institutions related to small urban manufacturers as prescribed by Presidential Decree.

(2) The SMBA administrator may provide financial assistance to cover the costs incurred by an entity designated according to the foregoing Paragraph (1) in conducting technological education and training.

(3) Necessary matters regarding the requirements and procedures to designate technical education and training institutes shall be prescribed by Presidential Decree.

Article 11 Termination of Designation As Technical Education and Training Institutes

If a technical education and training institute falls under any of the following, the SMBA administrator may terminate its designation thereas:

1. A technical education and training institute no longer satisfies the requirements for designation thereas;

2. A technical education and training institute requests termination of its designation thereas; or

3. A technical education and training institute uses financial assistance set forth in Article 10(2) hereof for any non-designated purpose.


Article 12 Selection of Outstanding Technicians

(1) The SMBA administrator may select outstanding technicians working for small urban manufacturers and award prizes to them.

(2) Necessary matters regarding the requirements and procedures to select outstanding technicians and provision of rewards for them under the foregoing Paragraph (1) shall be prescribed by Presidential Decree.


Article 13 Support for Technology Transfer

(1) The SMBA administrator shall endeavor to ensure transfer and development of small urban manufacturers' technologies.

(2) In order to support small urban manufacturers' technology transfer as provided in the foregoing Paragraph (1), the SMBA administrator may pursue any of the following undertakings:

1. Dissemination of excellent technologies and provision of technological information;

2. Transfer of excellent technologies through outstanding technicians under Article 12 hereof;

3. Provision of facilities and equipment for technology transfer;

4. Undertakings to encourage persons, to whom small urban manufacturers transfer their skills, to engage in the corresponding line of business for a long time; or

5. Other undertakings that the SMBA administrator deems necessary for technology transfer.


Article 14 Fosterage and Support of Outstanding Small Urban Manufacturers

(1) The SMBA administrator may choose small urban manufacturers heavily affecting

the regional economy by such means as local job creation and sales expansion or having the potential of advancing skills and engage in undertakings to support them with respect to any of the following:

1. Support for formulation of strategies to promote their growth into outstanding small urban manufacturers and to ensure their mid- to long-term development;

2. Dispatch and arrangement of experts by area including technology, human resources, finance, and business administration;

3. Provision of information to accelerate their growth into outstanding small urban manufacturers;

4. Guidance and advice concerning exploration of domestic and foreign markets; and

5. Other matters necessary to expedite their growth into outstanding small urban manufacturers.

(2) Necessary matters regarding selection and support of small urban manufacturers under the foregoing Paragraph (1) shall be prescribed by Presidential Decree.

## Chapter 4 Establishment of Foundation for Development of Small Urban Manufacturers

Article 15 Designation of Small Urban Manufacturer Cluster

(1) If necessary for development of small urban manufacturers, metropolitan city mayors and provincial governors may formulate a small urban manufacturer cluster promotion plan including each of the following and request the SMBA administrator to designate a certain part of the region under their jurisdiction (excluding an industrial complex as provided in Subparagraph 8, Article 2 of the Industrial Sites and Development Act) as a small urban manufacturer cluster (hereinafter referred to as "cluster"):

1. The area that wishes to be designated as a cluster;

2. The amount of financial resources required to promote a cluster and the method to secure such resources; and

3. Other matters prescribed by Presidential Decree to accelerate clustering of small urban manufacturers.

(2) If the SMBA administrator receives a request for designation of a cluster according to the foregoing Paragraph (1), he/she may designate a cluster by considering the feasibility of a cluster promotion plan and its harmony with the industrial site supply and demand plan under Article 5-2 of the Industrial Sites and Development Act, based on prior consultation with the heads of the central administrative agencies concerned. The same shall apply in the event of modification or termination thereof.

(3) If the SMBA administrator designates a cluster in accordance with the foregoing Paragraph (2), he/she shall make a public announcement thereof as prescribed by Presidential Decree.

Article 16 Financial Support for Small Urban Manufacturer Cluster

(1) For the development of small urban manufacturers, the SMBA administrator may grant preferential treatment to a local government having jurisdiction over a designated cluster in supporting the creation of a fund for the fosterage of local small and medium enterprises in accordance with Article 44(1) of the Balanced Regional Development and Support for Local Small and Medium Enterprises Act.

(2) The central government or local governments may grant small urban manufacturers located in or moving to a cluster preferential treatment in terms of financial assistance or other necessary matters.

(3) A person who falls under any of the following may preferentially issue a credit guarantee in order to help small urban manufacturers smoothly secure necessary funds in a cluster:

1. Credit guarantee funds under the Credit Guarantee Fund Act;

2. Korea Technology Credit Guarantee Fund under the Korea Technology Credit Guarantee Fund Act; and

3. Credit guarantee foundations established under Article 9 of the Regional Credit Guarantee Foundation Act.

Article 17 Infrastructure Establishment for Small Urban Manufacturer Cluster

(1) Metropolitan city mayors and provincial governors may execute any of the following undertakings in order to create and expand cluster infrastructure:

1. Installation of joint waste disposal facilities;

2. Improvement and repair of buildings and structures of the places of business;

3. Installation and improvement of joint warehouses, educational facilities, and safety facilities related to electricity, gas and fire;

4. Installation and repair of facilities and equipment to enhance convenience of the disabled, the aged and pregnant women in terms of transportation and use of the places of business and to provide them with easy access to information; and

5. Other undertakings necessary to build cluster infrastructure.

(2) The central government may provide financial assistance to cover the costs incurred to create and expand cluster infrastructure.

(3) Necessary matters regarding the support targets, limits, and procedures of the cluster infrastructure establishment project shall be prescribed by Presidential Decree.


Article 18 Establishment and Operation of Small Urban Manufacturer Support Center

(1) The SMBA administrator may establish and operate a small urban manufacturer support center (hereinafter in this article referred to as "support center") in order to render necessary support concerning development of small urban manufacturers and provision of technological information thereto:

(2) The support center shall perform each of the following duties:

1. Execution of projects to support small urban manufacturers including education and counseling;

2. Investigation and provision of technological information for small urban manufacturers;

3. Provision of services in alignment with other institutions and organizations rendering support for small urban manufacturers;

4. Provision of employment information and arrangement of jobs in relation to small urban manufacturers; and

5. Other undertakings necessary to support small urban manufacturers.

(3) The SMBA administrator may commission establishment and operation of the support center to a corporation or organization as prescribed by Presidential Decree.

(4) The support center shall have specialized staff satisfying the standards as prescribed by Presidential Decree to perform such affairs as education of and information provision to small urban manufacturers.

(5) The SMBA administrator may provide financial assistance to cover all or a part of the costs incurred by the support center in performing the affairs set forth in each subparagraph of the foregoing Paragraph (2).

(6) Necessary matters regarding establishment and operation of the support center shall be prescribed by Presidential Decree.


Article 19 Improvement of Places of Business and Working Environment

(1) The central and local governments may provide financial assistance necessary to improve the places of business and working environment of small urban manufacturers.

(2) The central and local governments may assess hazards concerning the working environment and characteristics of small urban manufacturers and render support necessary for improvement thereof.

(3) Necessary matters regarding the support targets, limits, procedures, and follow-up management of the business place and working environment improvement project shall be prescribed by Presidential Decree.


Article 20 Support for Joint Projects

The central and local governments may support any of the following joint projects for the purpose of curtailing management costs and expanding sales of small urban manufacturers:

1. Organization activities including establishment of a cooperative to perform joint projects;
2. Alignment between organizations (including corporations) set up to carry out joint projects and small and medium enterprises;
3. Projects related to product and design development and function improvement;
4. Projects related to joint facilities and equipment necessary for manufacturing;
5. Projects related to joint facilities and systems necessary for purchasing and logistics;
6. Projects related to joint market development including public relations and establishment of brands and stores; and
7. Other projects that the SMBA administrator deems necessary to support joint projects of small urban manufacturers.

Article 21 Establishment and Operation of Integrated Information System
(1) The SMBA administrator may build and operate an integrated information system so as to comprehensively manage information on small urban manufacturers and provide useful information to them.
(2) Necessary matters regarding the method and organization to operate the integrated information system under the foregoing Paragraph (1) shall be prescribed by Presidential Decree.

Article 22 Enhancement of Social Awareness
The central and local governments shall endeavor to increase social awareness of small urban manufacturers in order to improve public understanding of small urban manufacturers and develop social consensus on the importance of small urban manufacturers and their technologies.

## Chapter 5 Supplementary Provisions

Article 23 Delegation of Authority

*The SMBA administrator's authority hereunder may be partly delegated or entrusted, as prescribed by Presidential Decree, to the heads of central administrative agencies, metropolitan city mayors and provincial governors, city mayors, county heads and district heads (limited to the heads of autonomous districts), or the Small Enterprise and Market Service established under Article 17 of the Act on Protection and Support of Microenterprises. <Amended on January 28, 2015>*

Article 24 Hearing
The SMBA administrator shall hold a hearing in order to terminate designation as a technical education and training institute in accordance with Subparagraphs 1 and 3 of Article 11 hereof.

## Small Urban Manufacturers
Artisans of our times that Chun Soon-ok has ever met

First published 29 May 2015
English edition 20 April 2016

Written by Chun Soon-ok · Kwon Eun-jeong
Translated by Chun Soon-ok

Publisher  Jeong Jong-joo
Published in Korea by PURIWA IPARI(Root&Leaves) Publishing Co., Seoul

Registered   21 August 2001 No. 10-2201
Address      128-4 2F, World Cup-ro, Mapo-gu, Seoul, Korea
Tel          02)324-2142~3
Fax          02)324-2150
E-mail       puripari@hanmail.net

ISBN         978-89-6462-066-3 (03300)

Damaged book can be exchanged.
Book price is on the back page.